Hidden Identity of Women in Church and Society

Biblical Hermeneutics Rediscovered

The Series as the name suggests will focus on Biblical Hermeneutics, i.e., literary works concerned with methods of interpreting the Old and New Testaments of Bible via different stream of topics like Literature & Poetry, Indigenous Philosophizing, Ethical response towards Ecology, Health & Healing, Science & Technology, Feminist Theology, Sociological approach towards Human Rights, Law & Politics, Arts, History of Ideas, Ancient Civilizations, Cultural Contiguity, Religious Cosmologies & Mysticism, Appraisal of various Theologians, World Peace & Harmony, Global Capitalism, Network Marketing, Cybertheology, Population & Demographics, Epigraphic Studies, Contextualized Education, and many others. We welcome a Mss. on any topic/s mentioned, whether they are original works, scholarly monographs, collections of conference papers, revised dissertations, or translations of historical documents. Through the Series we, the Publishers, are striving to put forward published works that may help Institutions, Academic Bodies, Researchers, Scholars and the World at large in furthering their respective knowledge and understanding on the concerned subject. We welcome your comments on our efforts and further suggestions on how we can enshrine new ray of analysing & explaining the written texts through our upcoming books.

Biblical Hermeneutics Rediscovered - 2

Hidden Identity of Women in Church and Society

A Re-reading of the Book of Esther

Atula Ao

CWI

Christian World Imprints™

First Published in 2016 by

Christian World Imprints(TM)
Christian Publishing & Books from India
H-12 Bali Nagar, **New Delhi-110015**
info@christianworldimprints.com
www.ChristianWorldImprints.com
Phone: +91 11 25465925

ISBN 13: 978-93-5148-147-8 ISBN 10: 93-5148-147-6

Cataloging in Publication Data--DK
Courtesy: D.K. Agencies (P) Ltd. <docinfo@dkagencies.com>

Ao, Atula, 1972- **author.**
Hidden identity of women in church and society : a re-reading of the book of Esther / Atula Ao.
pages cm. -- (Biblical hermeneutics rediscovered ; 2)
Includes bibliographical references.
ISBN 9351481476
ISBN 9789351481478

1. Vashti, Queen of Persia. 2. Esther, Queen of Persia. 3. Women--Identity--Religious aspects--Christianity. 4. Women in the Bible. 5. Bible. Esther.--Criticism, interpretation, etc. I. Title. II. Series: Biblical hermeneutics rediscovered ; 2.

BS1375.52.A53 2016 DDC 222.906 23

Printed in India

Dedicated to my beloved parents
Mr. L. P. Asang
&
Mrs. M. Asangla
Without whose support, prayers and wishes I would not have been today what I am.

Contents

Foreword

I'm delighted and gratified to provide this Foreword to this book written by one of our emerging biblical scholars, whom I have had the pleasure of knowing as a student, mentor and now a colleague in the enterprise of theological education.

Identity formation is a constructive process; and there are often subtle influences that create (or recreate) human identities. Identity is an essential ingredient of human existence. It is both unique and common. However, generalization of identities can play a major role in the suppression of human dignity. It is from this prism, the identity of women both in India and elsewhere is often construed. "Women are weaker vessels;" "they are inferior, subordinate beings existing only for the pleasure and use of men;" etc., are the common notions (created) about women. Now, such entrenched identities are constructed and imposed by a patriarchal mind-set, which is so prevalent in our families, societies and even churches.

The author of the book, Dr. Atula Ao, picks up such a constructed identity of two women in the biblical narrative and tries to analyse it from the prism of women's identity formation, which in this case is a pure patriarchal construction. The story of the book of Esther is: the 'vamp' – Vashti versus the 'ideal' – Esther. Now, interestingly, these two identities are constructed and propagated by the patriarchal structures of the time. Intriguingly, these identities find a common platform even in the twenty-first century.

The author has rightly pointed out the importance of this study. She notes: many a times the scriptures (both Christian and others) are misinterpreted, misrepresented, misquoted, where some characters are highlighted, hyped up, whereas, many other (often very important ones) are ignored, hidden and negativised for obvious reasons. She points out that these are due to the influences of particular ideologies that are dominant in the context where it is written, and interpreted. The book of Esther is a vivid reflection of the inter-play of the dominant patriarchal ideology. It is also noted that such biblical texts are used as the basis for enforcing inferior and submissive roles to women both in the society and church. However, a re-reading of the biblical accounts from the feminist/womanist perspective helps in uncovering the different roles and contributions women have made in the Bible, which will empower the women today to break away from the clutches of patriarchal oppressions.

The author has clearly mentioned the purpose of this book: to understand the story of the Vashti and Esther in the Book of Esther, in a true light without any bias, to bring forward the true identity of Vashti and Esther, and to seek in depth the contribution of women in terms of the various roles they played in the society of their own times, and subsequently, to examine how these reinterpretations will enable a broader understanding of women in the society today.

There is an ardent need for more works on such issues from the Indian context and I am sure that this work will be an important asset to the growing number of biblical studies from Indian feminist/ womanist perspective. I warmly commend this book to the wider public with joy and a deep sense of gratitude.

Rev. Dr. J. R. John Samuel Raj
Principal
The United Theological College
&
Chairperson of the Academic Council
Senate of Serampore College (University)

Acknowledgements

The original work of this book: **"In Search of the Hidden Identity of Women : A Feminist Re-reading of the Book of Esther,"** was submitted to the Senate of Serampore College (University), India as a Master of Theology (Old Testament) thesis. The university has kindly granted the necessary permission to publish the same in a book form.

I am most grateful to my dissertation *guru* Rev. Dr. J. R. John Samuel Raj (Principal, United Theological College, Bangalore) for his time, encouragement, and expertise throughout this project. Without his constant help it would have been impossible for me to accomplish this great task. I am also thankful to him for writing the 'Foreword' for this book.

A very special thanks to Rev. Dr. Daniel Jones Muthunayagom, Rev. Dr. K. Jesurathanam from the Department of Old Testament studies and all my teachers and colleagues at United Theological College, Bangalore. A special word of thanks to my friends for their constant help and encouragement during my stay at Bangalore.

The constant prayers, encouragement and help of my dad and mom; my sister-Arenla, my brother-in-law Alongti Longchar and my brothers Mar and Lanu, have held my spirit high, thus making this research possible. They deserve words beyond gratitude.

I cannot put in words the amount of energy my husband, Dr. Samuel George has spent in making this work into a book form. He deserves a very big THANK YOU.

Special word of thanks to my home church-Mangmetong Baptist Church, Mokokchung, Nagaland, for their constant prayer support.

It is said, "When you absolutely positively have to know, go to a library." How true it is when it comes to research! I am thankful to the Library staffs at: United Theological College, Dharmaram Vidya Kshetram, St. Peter's Pontifical Seminary, SAIACS, all in Bangalore; Gurukul Lutheran Theological College, Chennai; and many other libraries around India.

A special word of appreciation to Christian World Imprints for transforming this research work into a book form.

A heartfelt thank you to all those who have prayed and wished me success all the way through my theological education. Thank you all.

List of Abbreviations

ABD	:	The Anchor Bible Dictionary
BDB	:	Brown Driver Briggs
BIB Rev	:	Bible Review
BIBLNT	:	Biblical Literature of New Testament
BTF	:	Bangalore Theological Forum
CBQ	:	Catholic Biblical Quarterly
ICC	:	The International Critical Commentary
JAAR	:	Journal of American Academy of Religion
JBL	:	Journal of Biblical Literature
JSOT	:	Journal for the Study of the Old Testament
VT	:	Vetus Testamentum
WBC	:	Word Biblical Commentary

Introduction

The issue of identity is a fundamental issue, for any individual precisely because humans are social beings, beings living in relation with other beings. The way one perceives herself/himself depends much on the way one is perceived by others in the society. To be recognized, as someone valuable is a basic human need, which in many occasions is even deeper than the physical needs of food, shelter and clothing.

The world we live in is changing rapidly due to intellectual, scientific and technological advancements. We witness new social movements, be it Dalit, Tribal, Feminist, Ecological or even movements against war and weapons. All these points out to the fact that issues of equality, justice, peace and harmony are important and are becoming more relevant for people all over the world. Consequently, this results in making the issue of identity significant, because these issues of equality, justice, peace and harmony are related either directly or indirectly to identity. In a community, often what a person's identity is perceived to be, decides his/her social standing, e.g., a Dalit, a Tribal, or a Woman are treated as subordinates because of what they represent. The identity that people have are not primarily created by a person, but rather it is influenced for the most part by what other people assume and assign identity to be.

Today, identity is conceived as self–identity and it operates through practices that are reflexive as well as rational. Identity is also concerned with individuals confronting the uncertainties and disembedding processes of modernity in their own lives and seeking some form of expression and identification with others.

1. Background of the Research

The Book of Esther is named after its heroine Esther. Throughout the century, the book is claimed to have given the historical origins of a Jewish festival. Traditionally, it is usually seen as the heroic tale of Esther against the Background of the disobedient Queen Vashti whom she replaces. In the case of Esther, we also see that patriarchy works by making her submit to their will, through which she is seen as a model for women. On the other hand, Vashti under the same situation is deposed from her royal throne due to her refusal to submit to the demands of the patriarchal society. The women are set against each other, and the one who obeys the rule of men is shown as representing a person of quality. On account of Vashti's deposition, many read this story as one of a disobedient queen and hence fail to discover and appreciate the courage and the challenge she displayed in disobeying the king's command.

Such interpretation points out that it involves issues that reflect a strong patriarchal hand in this book. Women were always kept under patriarchal and hierarchal concepts, which perceived them as inferior, subordinate beings existed only for the pleasure and use of men. At present women's identity is put to question, as women themselves and people at large become aware that identity is constructed socially, culturally and transferred through the communities' ideology.

At this point, biblical interpretation becomes an important issue because in the process of interpretation there exist of two elements; the interpreter's and the writer's frame of mind, and the context in which the Bible was written. Biblical texts are historically conditioned, and shaped by patriarchal society, thus they are patriarchal in nature. The biblical text undercuts the full humanity and equality of women by their illusions, their assertions or their omissions. Therefore, they must always be approached with suspicion. Consequently, interpreters have the responsibility of unmasking their patriarchal prejudice, whereby those aspects of the text that reinforce women to a secondary status must be exposed and reinterpreted.[1]

Therefore, this research is an investigation on the moral and ethical issues, which reflect a degrading role of women, particularly in the Persian society.

2. Significane of the Research

This research is important because, firstly, many a times the scriptures are misinterpreted, where certain aspects or characters are highlighted and hyped up, whereas other aspects or characters are ignored, hidden and negativised. This is the due to the influence of particular ideologies and concept which dominants the context in which it is interpreted. This component is vividly reflected in the Book of Esther. Secondly, such biblical texts are used as the basis for delineating women to submissive roles assigned by the patriarchal ideology. Thirdly, at present there is the need to uncover the different roles and contribution women have made in the Bible to break away from the stereotypical roles assigned to women, in order to empowering women struggle against oppression of patriarchy.

This research serves three perpose: to understand the story of the Vashti and Esther in the Book of Esther, in a true light without any bias, to bring forward the true identity of Vashti and Esther, and to seek in depth the contribution of women in terms of the various roles they played in the society of their own times, and subsequently, to examine how these reinterpretations will enable a broader understanding of women in the society today.

3. Methodology Adopted

This research is an attempt to bring out the true identity of Vashti and Esther who lived in a culture dominated by men, where they were forced to comply with the whims and fancies of men. It also endeavours to construe the identity of women today, by looking at how woman's body is socially and culturally constructed. Then

1 Alice L. Laffey, *Wives, Harlots and Concubines: The Old Testament in Feminist Perspectives* (Philadelphia: Fortress Press, 1988), 2-3.

consequently, a comparison will be made to bring out the identity of Esther and Vashti. Thus, re-reading these two identities in a reconstructive model.

The Book of Esther has been re-examined by using different hermeneutical approaches. Since for long, Vashti has been condemned and shown by the writers and interpreters of the scripture as a negative model for women. Esther is also interpreted as a mere puppet in the hands of men, whose only attribute is said to be her beauty. The book attempts to bring out a positive identity of Vashti and Esther. Thus, it will throw light on the various elements that influence one's interpretation of the scripture, and take up the story of Vashti and Esther, and apply to it the methodology of Feminist hermeneutics.

The research will mainly deal from the point of women's concern. It will focus on how the Book of Esther has come to be written, what kind of society it reflects, why certain things were interpreted in the way it is seen, and how the women mentioned in the book played an important part. Furthermore, the work will reflect in particular, how the status of women has been confined to as a mere sex object, and how even today this tag is confining women within its narrow scope.

This Exegetical study has a clear focus on the Book of Esther, and particularly on the first and second chapters of the book. The tools used are Form criticism, Traditio-Historical criticism and Feminist hermeneutics. Elizabeth Schüssler Fiorenza's method of Feminist hermeneutics was the main tool of the research. The research is limited to library work – Books, Journals, and Articles.

The book contains four chapters including Introduction and Conclusion. The introductory chapter highlights the rationale of the chosen topic and methodology used in the research.

The first chapter explores the different methods of Feminist reading of the Bible, dealing in brief its historical development, and its methodologies. Further more, the Feminist methodology applied, is laid down with special emphasis on the Feminist hermeneutics of Elizabeth Schüssler Fiorenza.

The second chapter highlights the historical, political, and social background of the Book of Esther, keeping in mind the patriarchal power at play in its composition.

The third chapter probes deep into the search for the hidden identity of Vashti and Esther, by exegeting selected verses, and reinterpreting them with a purpose of uncovering their suppressed identity.

The fourth chapter examines how society and culture constructs the identity of women as a body. It further brings out in its implications for re-reading the construction of Esther and Vashti, and also the identity of women in general.

The concluding chapter sums up the arguments of the preceding chapters, and brings out the liberative motive of moving away from interpreting women as mere objects. Thus, proposing an identity of equality.

Chapter 1

Feminist Reading of the Bible

How should the Bible be read when the Bible clearly teaches a subordinate role for women? Some christians chose to ignore what the Bible says about women, since it was written 2000 years ago, and therefore not relevant to our times. Some chose to reinterpret it, while others choose not to move away from traditional interpretations. According to Katharine Doob Sakenfeld, "the challenge of feminist biblical interpretation is to find another way, another approach that finds new ground, neither accepting blindly traditional interpretation nor ignoring the Bible as useless ancient document."[1] She further states that, one great advantage of using the Bible in a general way rather than just concentrating on the texts that specifically mention women, is that, feminist interpretation can move beyond being just reactive to those who want to continue patriarchy, and instead make a positive and constructive emphasis on *shalom*, wholeness or salvation in the broadest and deepest sense of the term. It offers a basis for the solidarity of the whole human community by questioning the needs

1 Katharine Doob Sakenfeld, "Feminist Reading of the Bible: Problems and Promises," *Bangalore Theological Forum* XXXII (Dec. 2000), 19.

of one group over the other.[2] But, this statement does not represent how the Bible is read; different feminist scholars have put forward different approaches in view of its interpretation.

This chapter attempts to present the main ideas and concepts behind the feminist reading of the Bible. It looks into development of the term, and the reasons behind its development, and basically at what it aims. It further explains the different hermeneutical process that is involved in feminist reading.

1.1. Issues involved in Biblical Hermeneutics

The Bible can be used either as an instrument of domination, or for liberation. Biblical interpretation is never only limited to religious matter, but is rather extended to the whole process of formation, canonization and transmission of the Bible that have always been soaked with the issues of authority and power.[3] Historical-critical method-employs all the tools of historical criticism, and then seeks to mediate, translate, and interpret the meaning into their present horizon.[4]

The formation of both the Old and the New Testaments was a social event of the faith of the communities. The writers acted as the representatives of these faith communities, and their concern was to articulate the faith of their community and at the same time, making use of their own thinking and literary skills.[5] The writers and interpreters even today cannot escape from the dominant ideology of their community. The meaning of a piece of writing is seldom clearly self-evident. This is especially true in the case of the Bible that is written by people who lived in a very different cultural and historical setting. The meaning of the words used at the time of the writing, the

2 Katharine Doob Sakenfeld, "Feminist Reading of the Bible: Problems and Promises," *Bangalore Theological Forum* XXXII (Dec. 2000), 24.

3 Kwok Pui-Lan, *Discovering the Bible in the Non-Biblical World* (Maryknoll: Orbis Books, 1995), 8-9.

4 Robert Grant & David Tracy, A *Short History of the Interpretation of the Bible* (Philadelphia: Fortress Press, 1984), 159-160.

5 Joseph Pathrapankal, *Text and Context: In Biblical Interpretation* (Bangalore: Dharmaram Publication, 1993), 7.

purpose of the author's writing, and its application for the believers in the contemporary church form important questions.[6]

All understanding requires a framework or context within which interpretation is to take place; it cannot be limited to the grammatical–historical techniques if interpreters are to understand the original meaning of the text.[7] The meaning of a text is not exhausted by what the author intended or what the text says, whether the author explicitly intended it or not. But, it is also what the readers today understand as part of the dynamic meaning of the text within their own historical, cultural and religious context.[8] The Bible becomes the word of God when it speaks and inspires in us a positive change.[9] Therefore, biblical hermeneutics is not just sitting and reading what the text says as right, but investigating and exploring in depth to find out the how's, and why's of a particular text.

Women were treated as mere properties of men in the environments where the Bible came into being and interpreted.This is still true today, in the interpretation process.The scripture has its limitation in its social settings and contexts. Power is involved in interpretation process. The interpretation of the Bible reflects the western dualistic understanding of human nature and destiny.[10] Thus reinterpretation requires breaking away from such ideologies and constructions that degrade women, and seeking new perspectives which empower women.

1.2. Definition of Feminism

The word 'feminist' generally describes, the aspiration to eliminate women's subordination and marginalization. A 'feminist' is one who

---

6 David S. Dockery, *Christian Scripture: An Evangelical Perspective on Inspirations, Authority and Interpretation* (Nashville: Broadman & Holman Publisher, 1995), 159.

7 *Ibid.*

8 Pathrapankal, *Text and Context: In Biblical Interpretation*, 6.

9 For the text to become alive and be useful for us, it must have the capability to give strength and meaning to one's life and struggles.

10 Kwok Pui-Lan, *Discovering the Bible in the Non-Biblical World,* 11.

seeks justice and equality for all people, and especially concerning itself with the fate of women - all women - in the midst of 'all people.' Such a definition addresses issues pertinent to racism, classism, and ecology, as well as peacemaking, as part of the interest and range of feminism.[11]

Varied articulations of feminism can be found, but generally they agree in their critique of masculine domination, and hold that gender roles are socially constructed rather than innate. Feminist analysis often utilises categories such as patriarchy, androcentrism or gender dualism as synonymous or overlapping concepts. Patriarchy is generally defined as gender dualism or as the domination of man over woman.[12]

1.3. Brief History of the Development of the Different Feminist Readings

The women's liberation movement first began in the United States, in the context of the fight against slavery, and then, in the latter struggles for racial equality. Women started questioning their assigned role and function in the church and society, given to them by men. This resulted in the re-examination of many biblical passages, and a dynamic process of interpreting the scripture from a feminist perspective, which has questioned and challenged many of the traditional male interpretation of the text.[13]

Although the feminist interpretation developed in recent years as a distinct discipline of the Bible, its history can be traced back to the 18th century. Hubertin Auclert is credited as the first person to use the word ' Feminism' in 1882, associating it with the struggle

11 Katharine Doob Sakenfeld, "Feminist Perspectives on Bible and Theology: An Introduction to Selected Issues and Literature," *Interpretation: A Journal of Bible and Theology* XLII, no. 1 (Jan. 1998), 5.

12 Elisabeth Schüssler Fiorenza, "Feminist Hermeneutics," *ABD,* Vol. 2, ed. D. N. Freedman (New York: Double Day, 1992), 784.

13 Joseph Abraham, *Re-reading the Old Testament: A Study of Feminist Readings of Gen 1-3,* A Thesis Submitted in Partial Fulfillment of the University's Requirement for the Degree of the Doctor of Philosophy, July 1996, Coventry University in Collaboration with Wycliffe Hall, Oxford, England, 1.

of women in gaining political rights.[14] This term first appeared in 1895 in a British journal named, *The Athenaeum* in April 27th.[15] Women by this time were generally aware of their place and role in the society, and church than ever before. They therefore, started thinking critically about the status assigned to them by the male world and started questioning the traditional scriptural interpretations concerning their societal and ecclesiastical roles.[16]

In the context of feminist movement in the last century feminists began to explore the implications and possibilities of biblical interpretation that takes the patriarchal character into account. There are many types of feminist hermeneutics. Carolyn De Swarte Gifford shows that the first type of feminist reading to appear in the 19th century was proof texting. Women's struggles for empowerment in 19th century discovered passages supportive of women, which they could use to counter the biblical passages quoted by those who wished to keep women in their place. Towards the end of the 19th century, under the leadership of Elizabeth Cady Stanton feminist critical assessment of the biblical text as sexist began.[17] Stanton found it necessary to engage in the interpretation of the Bible because, it was used as the ultimate approval against any change in conditions for women.

Taken together these approaches could be called the first stage of feminist hermeneutics. In the 20th century more complex and sophisticated types of feminist hermeneutics have developed. Fiorenza proposes three fold approaches to the Bible, firstly, its sexist characteristics should be pointed out and rejected as being unauthoritative. Secondly, by using the methods developed by

---

14 Anne M. Clifford, *Introducing Feminist Theology* (Maryknoll: Orbis Books, 2001), 11.

15 Alice S Rossi, "Preface: Feminist Lives and Works," in *The Feminist Papers: From Adams to De Beauvior*, ed. A. S Rossi (New York & London: Columbia University Press, 1973), xii-xiii.

16 Abraham, *Re-reading the Old Testament: A Study of Feminist Readings of Gen 1-3*, 34.

17 Adela Yarbro Collins, "Introduction," *Feminist Perspectives on Biblical Scholarship,* ed. Adela Yarbro Collins (Chico: Scholar Press, 1985), 4.

feminist historians, the virtually invisible women are written back into the biblical text. Thirdly, Bible is to be used for empowering by lifting and proclaiming women.[18]

Fiorenza in her presidential address (1987) to the Society of Biblical Literature said:

> If scripture text have served not only noble causes but also to legitimate war, to nurture anti-Judaism and misogynism, to justify the exploitation of slavery, and to promote colonial dehumanisation, then biblical scholarship must take the responsibility not only to interpret biblical text in their historical context but also to evaluate the construction of their historical words and symbolic universes in terms of a religious scale of values. [19]

Phyllis Trible put forward three approaches in feminist hermeneutics and biblical studies. According to her, the reading engages scripture in three ways, firstly it cites, and devaluates long neglected data that show the inferiority, subordination, and abuse of the female in ancient and early church. The second approach, discerns within the Bible critics of patriarchy, upholding forgotten text and reinterpreting familiar ones, to shape a remnant theology that challenges the sexism of scripture. The third approach incorporates the other two recounting tales of terror in memoriam, to offer sympathetic readings of abused women.[20] Her work exemplifies the approach to rhetorical criticism.

Fiorenza concentrates on historical reconstruction of the life and practice of the earliest Christian Communities; Bernadette Brooton examines inscriptional evidence for the role of women in early

---

18 Elisabeth Schüssler Fiorenza, *In Memory of Her: A Feminist Theological Reconstruction of Christian Origins,* Tenth Anniversary Edition (New York: Cross Roads, 2002), xvi.

19 Elisabeth Schüssler Fiorenza, "The Ethics of Biblical Interpretation: De Centering Biblical Scholarship," *JBL* 107 (1988): 15.

20 Phyllis Trible, *Texts of Terror: Literary Feminist Readings of Biblical Narratives* (Philadelphia: Fortress Press, 1984), 3.

synagogues;[21] Carol Meyers examines archaeological remains and cross-cultural patterns of socio-economic organization in studying the sex roles and attitudes of pre-monarchic Israelites.[22]

The present influx of feminist materials itself shows this topic has become important in biblical research. Therefore, it is important to evaluate the feminist contribution to Old Testament studies. J.W. Rogerson rightly points out that "the future existence of the Old Testament studies depends upon how it reacts to the questions that are being put to it by liberation hermeneutics, and the enterprise culture."[23]

Social location influenced the lives recorded in the Bible, and as such, every reader is influenced by his or her social location. This can be seen clearly in the third wave feminist movement. African-American women at present read the scripture in a context shaped by the history and experiences of slavery. Thus, they use the term 'Womanist' which names African-American women's resistance to oppression as well as their self-affirmation and the will to survive with human dignity. The Bible which was cited by Europeans and Euro-American Christians to legitimate the enslavement of the ancestors of African-American is also a source of religious validation and liberation in the lives of black women.[24]

---

21 Bernadette Brooton, *Brown Judaic Studies* (Chico: Scholars Press, 1982), 36.

22 Carol Meyers, "Procreation, Production, and Protection: Male-Female Balance in Early Israel," *JAAR* 51(1983), 569-593.

23 J. W. Rogerson, "What does it Mean to be Human? The Central Question of Old Testament Theology," *JSOT* 87 (1990), 298.

24 Clifford, *Introducing Feminist Theology*, 79.
This term 'womanist' was coined by Alice Walker the author of "The Color Purple." It appeared first in "*In our Mother's Garden: Womanist Movement,*" published in 1983. She maintains that womanist is to feminist what purple is to violet. Cf. Gabriele Dietrich, *A New Thing on Earth: Hopes and Fears Facing Feminist Theology* (Delhi: ISPCK, 2001), 234. This thesis does not aim to dwell on the difference between 'Womanist' and 'Feminist'. It will use the word 'Feminist' to understand the situation of women in their oppressive and marginalized state. This word is preferred to study the biblical and historical constructed status of women in the Book of Esther.

Feminist hermeneutics shares the major characteristics of liberation hermeneutics. This hermeneutics has both theoretical and practical goal. The praxis-orientation locates feminist hermeneutics in the context of philosophical and theological hermeneutics, as well as, critical theory and liberation theology.[25] David J. A. Clines also points out that feminist criticism calls "great promise for biblical interpretation, as well as also on the other theological disciplines."[26] The main task of a critical feminist hermeneutics is not to defend biblical authority, but to articulate the theological authority of women.[27]

The concept that understanding is not a simple process but that each word, language, and meaning has complexity because of the influence of dominant ideology or culture, has helped feminists prove the need for interpreting the scripture from their perspectives and for their needs. Although, the tools and approaches differ among the feminist scholars, the essence of feminist hermeneutics is the empowerment of women by bringing out new interpretation that put women in new light, minus those concepts that marginalise them.

1.4. Feminist Hermeneutics

According to Adela Yarbro Collins, feminist hermeneutics may be defined as interpreting the texts with the principle of feminism in mind. More realistically, it is the business of reading texts with sensitivity to sexist oppression.[28] Trible defines it as "a critique of culture in light of misogyny."[29] Renita Weems writes " A challenge for marginalised readers in general, and African-American women in

25 Elisabeth Schüssler Fiorenza, *Bread not Stone: The Challenges of Feminist Biblical Interpretation* (Boston: Beacon Press, 1995), 2.

26 D. J. Clines, "Possibilities and Priorities of Biblical Interpretation in an International Perspectives," *BIBLNT 1*(1993), 83.

27 Fiorenza, *In Memory of Her: A Feminist Theological Reconstruction of Christian Origins*, 108.

28 Adela Yarbro Collins, *Helpmates, Harlots, Heroes: Women's Stories in the Hebrew Bible* (Louisville: Westminster John Knox Press, 1994), 14.

29 Phyllis Trible, *God and the Rhetoric of Sexuality* (Philadelphia: Fortress Press, 1978), 7.

particular, has been to use whatever means necessary to recover the voice of the oppressed within biblical texts."[30]

Biblical interpretation seeks to understand the text and its world as a rhetorical expression in a certain historical situation. This is seen in Hans-Georg Gadamer who talks about the authority of the text as resting on recognition *(Anerkennung),* because the subject matter of the text can be accepted in principle.[31] Interpretation as its goal has to establish agreement to and acceptance of the subject matter of the text. Bible has been accepted as a source of norm of inspiration throughout the centuries with the message of God's act of liberation in history. However, today feminist theologians question the Bible as having androcentric languages and characters that dominates and oppresses women in the text. Therefore, a re-reading of the Bible is in order to reclaim it as normative and authoritative. Rather than relinquishing its androcentric language, they seek to reconstruct the history of women and reclaim women's biblical heritage.[32] Feminist biblical interpretation seeks not only to understand but also to assess critically the meaning of androcentric texts, and their socio-political functions. This is done by engaging in theological critique, evaluation, and transformation of biblical traditions and interpretations that provide an advantage to its particular socio-political and religious location.

In interpretation of the androcentric texts as informative and objective, reports of events and histories are taken. These texts are understood as social constructions by men and for men. Thus there

30 Renita Weems, "Reading her Way through the Struggle: African-American Women and the Bible," *Stony the Road we Trod: African Biblical Interpretation*, ed., Cain Hope Felder (Minneapolis: Fortress Press, 1991), 73.

31 In so far as the interpreter always approaches biblical texts with certain pre-understandings, and from within a definite linguistic-historical tradition, the act of interpretation has to overcome the distance between the world of the text and that of the interpreter in a 'fusion of horizons.' Cf. Hans-Georg Gadamer, *Truth and Method* (New York: Crossroad, 1989), 369-379.

32 Rosemary Radford Ruether, *Sexism and God Talk: Towards a Feminist Theology* (Boston: Beacon Press, 1983), 31.

is the need to read the 'silences' of women, which are not indicated by the text directly.[33]

1.5. Feminist Hermeneutical Approaches

Feminists have evolved polyvalent approaches to reading the Bible. A critical feminist hermeneutics of liberation focuses on the process of biblical interpretation that can fight the oppressive elements and at the same time, work as a liberating function in women's lives and struggles. Their overall method is essentially an individual's theological perspective on the biblical traditions that determines ones hermeneutical approach to the text.[34] Jonathan Culler classifies feminist reading process into three 'levels' or 'moments.'[35] At the first 'level,' the criticism is focused on the concern of the woman character and her experiences. The second 'level' of feminist criticism aims to make readers - men and women - question the liberating and political assumptions on which their readings has been based. In the third 'level,' women readers explore alternative readings.[36]

According to Fiorenza, a feminist reading of the Bible requires both transformation of our patriarchal understandings of God, scripture, and the church as well as transformation in the self-understanding of Historical-Critical scholarship, and the theological disciplines.[37] Focusing on the process of hermeneutics within the circle of feminist hermeneutics, the various hermeneutics can be as follows:

---

33 Elisabeth Schüssler Fiorenza, "Remembering the Past in Creating the Future: Historical-Critical Scholarship and Feminist Biblical Interpretation," *Feminist Perspectives on Biblical Scholarship,* 60.

34 Some presuppose that the Bible is permeated with patriarchy and therefore develop a rejectionist stance. On the other hand, some still believe that the Bible itself can offer a critique of patriarchal domination and hence develop a revisionary approach. Cf. Joseph Abraham, *Re-reading the Old Testament: A Study of Feminist Readings of Gen 1-3*, 41.

35 Jonathan Culler, *On Deconstruction: Theory and Criticism after Structuralism* (London: Routledge & Kegars Paul, 1983), 43-64.

36 *Ibid.*, 51.

37 Elisabeth Schüssler Fiorenza, *Bread Not Stone*, V-XVII.

1.5.1. *Hermeneutics of Experience*

Experience[38] of women becomes the starting point of feminist hermeneutics. This comes from an awareness that the experience of women have been neglected and marginalised. In the spheres of religion and spirituality women's experiences are that of exclusion and silencing. The experiences of women include not only of the contemporary women, but also of the biblical women.[39]

Feminist hermeneutics aims at conscientization and emancipation, which begins with the hermeneutics of experience. Feminists insist that women are 'scripted' and at the same time are historical subjects and agents.[40] All knowledge is seen as controlled by a male bias, formulated by them, for their benefits. Thus, the only way to fight this is to search for concepts beyond these male accepted and defined concepts.

---

38 "Women's experience explodes as a critical force, exposing classical theology, including its foundational tradition in scripture, as shaped by male experience rather than human experience. It throws a universality of the claims of the tradition into question." Cf. Rosemary Radford Ruether, "Feminist Interpretation: A Method of Correlation," *Feminist Interpretation of the Bible*, ed. Letty M. Russell (Philadelphia: Westminster Press, 1985), 113.

39 This calls feminists to listen to the voices of oppression and liberation. Christian feminist theology starts with naming these experiences of marginalisation and articulating women's experience of the divine norm of experience with four components: First of all experience is mediated linguistically and culturally. Secondly, individual experiences are not private but public and are affected by variables of class, gender, caste, and race and so on in its construction. Thirdly, since experience is determined socially and religiously it calls for an analysis. Finally, experience is the starting point and not a norm. Cf. Elisabeth Schüssler Fiorenza, *Wisdom Ways: Introducing Feminist Biblical Interpretation* (Maryknoll: Orbis Books, 2001), 169.

40 Feminist scholars utilize women's experience of reality and practical activity as a scientific resource and a major pointer of the reality against which hypotheses are to be tested. A critical feminist version of objectivity recognizes the provisionality and multiplicity of particular knowledge as situated and embodied knowledge. Understanding that knowledge is not totally relative and is possible from the perspective of the excluded and dominated to give a more adequate account of the 'world.' Cf. Elisabeth Schüssler Fiorenza, "Feminist Hermeneutics," *ABD* Vol. 2, 786.

Women's experiences are different from that of men, and it is because of their experiences of oppression and marginalisation that they seek liberation. Therefore, the process of hermeneutics has to start from their experiences because the only way to fight an element is to first understand what it is.

1.5.2. *Hermeneutics of Domination and Social Location*

Hermeneutics of social location critically reflects on both the social location of the interpreter and the text, and also on the relation of domination operating in the society. Asking questions about one's social location and participation, we become conscious of our self-identity as members of a community. A hermeneutics of domination makes it possible to understand how one acts in a specific situation, how we express ourselves in seeking the transformation from socially defined categories of domination.[41]

A feminist hermeneutics insist on a systematic analysis, with the aim that will both separate the ideological and theological functions of the biblical texts that legitimate Kyriarchy,[42] and also set free the potential within biblical texts to foster justice and liberation. Such analysis identifies both contemporary situations of domination and situations inscribed in the biblical texts.

This hermeneutics is important because through this we can identify those elements that oppress women, whether it is in the social, political, cultural or in the religious life. This further leads one to understand which issues need to be addressed and why. The scripture as book was formulated under the bias of patriarchy and reflects its biases because of the socio-political and cultural life

41 Fiorenza, *Wisdom Ways*, 172-175.

42 A neologism coined by E. S. Fiorenza. It is derived from the Greek word for "Lord" or "master"(*Kyrios*) and "to rule and dominate" (*Archein*) which seeks to redefine the analytic category of patriarchy in terms of multiplicative intersecting structures of domination. Kyriarchy is a socio-political system of domination in which elite educated propertied men hold poiwer over women and other men. Kyriarchy is best theorized as a complex pyramid system of intersecting multiplicative social structures of superordination, of ruling and oppression. Cf. Elisabeth Schüssler Fiorenza, *Wisdom Ways,* 211.

of the biblical times. Thus, to study how far this acts as a bias in interpretation is important.

1.5.3. *Hermeneutics of Suspicion*

The hermeneutics of suspicion[43] can be defined as a deconstructive practice of inquiry that denaturalises and demystifies linguistic and cultural practices of domination, rather than as working away at the layers of cultural sediments that hide or repress a deeper truth. Hermeneutics of suspicion investigates the dominant ideology behind the text.[44]

Fiorenza advances the term feminist hermeneutics of suspicion in developing such interpretative observation for explicit feminist historical reconstruction and theology by pointing out the underlying presuppositions and androcentrism in the scripture.[45] Fiorenza develops from it a 'dualistic hermeneutical strategy.' [46] She proposed two critical moments leading to a hermeneutics of suspicion - a consciousness - raising and a systematic analysis that arises from conscientization.[47]

---

43 This hermeneutics learns to recognize socio-political, economic, cultural and religious contradictions and from cognitive dissonance recognizing the gap between experience and personal values on the one hand and text and interpretation that deviate from or exclude lived experiences. Suspicion, is aroused by the insights that all biblical texts are articulated in grammatically masculine language. It challenges and demystifies the structures of domination that are inscribed in the biblical text, in our experience and in contemporary contexts of interpretation.

44 Fiorenza, *Wisdom Ways*, 175.

45 Fiorenza, *Bread Not Stone*, 15-17.

46 Fiorenza locates two contradictory facts concerning women in the Bible: on the one hand the Bible has promoted patriarchal and androcentric values, yet on the other hand, the Bible serves to inspire and authorize women and other non-persons in their struggles against patriarchal oppression. Cf. Elisabeth Schüssler Fiorenza, "Transforming the Legacy of Women's Bible," *Searching the Scripture: A Feminist Introduction*, Vol.1, ed., E. S. Fiorenza (London: SCM Press, 1994), 1-24.

47 First used by Paulo Freire in *Pedagogy of the Oppressed* (New York: Herder & Herder, 1971). 78.

In the encounter between text and readers, the reader's presuppositions and familiarity with other materials, experiences, community, desire influence either consciously or subconsciously in the construction of meaning. Problems arise when readers find contradictions and inconsistency in the scripture.[48] Thus, a hermeneutics of suspicion firstly makes a critical analysis of dominant strategies of meaning making. Secondly, it draws out and makes superior/inferior, we/others roles and values inscribed in the text. Thirdly, it articulates the ideological strategies of the text. Fourthly, it makes apparent the text's interaction and resonance with our experience and cultural value system. Ultimately, it seeks to determine and circumscribe the rhetorical situation and context in which the text was formulated and operates today.[49] Once the knowledge is perceived as having biases it prompts one to look at it suspiciously, which does not mean that we oppose to what is written, but to understand the ideology behind the text and how it has been interpreted.

1.5.4. *Hermeneutics of Recuperation*

According to the Postmodern Bible this hermeneutics is interpreted as, "the hermeneutics of recuperation remains thoroughly invested in the economic of truth and offers no critique of the philosophical grounds of the Bible's true claims."[50] Phyllis A. Bird methodology

48 According to Hans-George Gadamer one can understand the text only when the text speaks and answer us the words of one's own language. Cf. Hans-George Gadamer, *Philosophical Hermeneutics*, trans.& ed. David E. Linge (California: University of California Press, 1976), 57. According to F. D. E. Schleiermacher there are problems of language because there exist a plurality of meanings for a particular word. Cf. F. D. E. Schleiermacher, *Hermeneutic: The Handwritten Manuscripts*, trans. J. Duke & J. Forstman, ed. Heinz Kimmerle, (Missoula, Montana: Scholars Press, 1977), 70-73.

49 Fiorenza, *Bread Not Stone,* 176-177.

50 George Aichele et al. ed., *The Postmodern Bible* (London: Yale University Press, 1995), 246.

is based on the Traditional-Historical Criticism, through which she attempts to recover the "hidden history of women." [51]

In hermeneutics of recuperation the interpreter first aims to recover the biblical texts from patriarchal mistranslations and misinterpretations. Through their reading they attempt to 'reclaim' the text as positive to women. Trible, finds the 'depatriarchalising principle' at work in the scripture itself against the patriarchal culture. She writes "I affirm that the internationality of biblical faith, as distinguished from a general description of biblical religion, is neither to create nor to perpetuate patriarchy, but rather to function as salvation for both women and men."[52] Her method is that of re-reading to depatriarchalising the text. Trible and others[53] have attempted to re-read the famous text used against women (Gen.1-3),[54] by employing a hermeneutics of retrieval to bring into focus women's role model from the Old Testament.

J. Cheryl Exum adapted a literary critical analysis in her feminist exegesis, and has done a great deal of research on literary approaches to the Bible. By reopening the prevailing patriarchal nature of the scripture, she brings out counter pictures through the process of close reading (e.g. The women of Exodus, Ruth, Esther, Judith). Such readings provide recognition of the prevailing patriarchal nature of the scripture. Consequently, Exum through this method provides

51 She has contributed many articles in the area of woman's studies in Early Israel and their position in the Israelite cult. Further, Trible has also attempted to 'recover a neglected history' thereby offering a hermeneutics of remembrance. E. S. Fiorenza criticizes Trible for her neo-orthodox theology, claiming that "A biblical theology that does not seriously confront 'the patriarchal stamp' of the Bible and its religious–political legitimization of the patriarchal oppression of women is in danger of using a feminist perspective to rehabilitate the authority of the biblical history and theological heritage." Cf. Phyllis A. Bird, "Images of Women in the Old Testament," *The Bible and Liberation*, ed. Norman Gottwald (New York), 250-306. Also see, Iiana Pardes, *Counter Traditions in the Bible: A Feminist Approach* (London: Harvard University Press, 1993), 21.

52 Phyllis Trible, "Depatriarchalizing in Biblical Interpretation," *JAAR* XLI, no. 1(March 1973): 37.

53 Phyllis Bird, Joy Elasky, Fleming, and Mary Evans.

54 Mary J. Evans, *Women in the Bible* (Carlisle: Paternoster Press, 1983), 11-20.

"positive portrayals of women."[55] She writes, "within the patriarchal context of the biblical literature, we find strong countercurrents of affirmation of women: stories that show women's courage, strength, faith, ingenuity, talents, dignity and worth."[56]

1.5.5. *Hermeneutics of Creative Imagination*

A hermeneutics of imagination offers the possibility of imagining a new world of justice and well-being. It helps us to tell the story differently, in a way other than the kyriarchal stories of exclusion. This strategy employs aesthetic methods like role-play, bibliodrama, pictorial arts, dance, story telling and so on. However, all these methods are to be coupled with the hermeneutics of critical evaluation and suspicion, so that retellings of scripture will not re-inscribe cultural and stereotypical notions of women.

1.5.6. *Hermeneutics of Resistance*

Many Postmodern feminist readings apply hermeneutics of resistance. Resistance reading demonstrates the fundamental openness of a text and how meaning cannot be determined absolutely, but is itself resistant to ultimate or final interpretation.[57]

In the hermeneutics of resistance the reading strategy which is applied by the various feminists are the different hermeneutical

55 J. Cheryl Exum, "You shall let Every Daughter Live: A Study of Exodus 1: 8-2:10," *The Bible and Feminist*, ed. M. A. Tolbert (Chico: Scholars Press, 1983), 63-82.

56 J. Cheryl Exum, "The Mothers of Israel: The Patriarchal Narratives from a Feminist Perspective," *BIB Rev 2* (1986): 60.

57 Sarah Gamble, *The Routledge Companion to Feminism and Post Feminism*, (London & New York: Routledge, 2001), 44.

methods such structuralism,[58] Literary criticism,[59] Semiotics,[60] Psycho-analytic criticism,[61] Deconstruction[62] and Intertextuality.[63]

The feminist reading of Mieke Bal, Ilana Pardes, Danna Nolan Fewell, Pamela J. Milne, and Athalya Brenner all project to some degree or other kind of resistant reading. All these feminists analyse the Hebrew Bible as a thoroughly patriarchal construct, and develop a strategy of response and resistance, and in some case offer counter reading. Brenner writes at length as a Jewish woman both in Hebrew and in English. She examines the social roles of Israelite women by a literary normative approach. Her study reveals the various roles

58 It searches the deep structures encoded within the text itself, by combining linguistic theory and anthropological research. It perceives human reality as deep structure with an unconscious mythic pattern of meaning, having ontological significance. The task of structural exegesis is the decoding of texts to disclose its structures.

59 It critically analysis the literary features like, distinct style, vocabulary, theological features, the origin (authorship), date, and the purpose for which a particular text was written and determined.

60 Its mode is particularly to the fore in poetic language, manifested in rhythm, syntactic irregularities and linguistic distortions like metaphor and metonymy. Cf. Sarah Gamble, *The Routledge Companion to Feminism and Post Feminism*, 311.

61 Phyllis Chester's groundbreaking work with women patients in the early 70's argued that Psychoanalysis regards sickness as a normative characteristic of feminity. Men's fear of women is determined psychoanalytically by women's domination of childcare, while Kate Millet claimed that the definitions and practices of psychoanalysis were innately sexist. Cf. *Ibid.*, 300.

62 Structuralism, post-structuralism, deconstruction are tightly knotted. Deconstruction is a dismantling of structures (philosophical, cultural. political, institutional and above all and from the start textual, that was designed to show how they were put together in the first place. Deconstruction is text-centered Deconstruction makes explicit what is hidden, repressed or denied in any ordinary reading. Cf. Aichele et al.,*The Postmodern Bible,* 121.

63 A term introduced by Julia Kristeva which suggests that each texts is situated for each reader in an ever changing web composed of innumerable texts. There is no extra textual reality to which texts refer or which gives texts their meaning; meaning or reference are possibly only in relation to this network, as functions of intertextuality. *Ibid.*, 130.

taken by women in the Old Testament period. She concludes that women always have a secondary status in Israelite society.[64]

1.5.7. *Hermeneutics of Remembrance and Reconstruction*

To remember, means to bring together different parts of a larger structure, in order to construct a new design. In this case, the different elements are the surviving bits and pieces of women's forgotten and petite histories. Thus the hermeneutics of remembering widens our historical imagination.

A hermeneutics of remembrance reclaims the suffering and struggles of the past, proposing theoretical models that place women in the centre of biblical community and theology. Its primary task is to reclaim women's biblical heritage.[65] It searches the Bible and draws attention to women who have had little significance through out the christian tradition and history, by identifying and uncovering patriarchal biases. Through this search, these women's stories are used to empower women in their process of liberation.[66] This works to increase the distance between the present reader and the time of the text and to increase one's historical knowledge and imagination.[67]

The biblical women have been silenced by patriarchy, by either neglecting to mention them, or by not attributing any importance to them or even by overlooking them. A hermeneutics of remembrance searches and brings those forgotten, nameless, neglected stories of women, so that their stories may come alive today and their contributions and struggles in the community be made known. A hermeneutics of reconstruction allows women to enter the biblical story through historical imagination, artistic recreation and liturgical ritualisation.[68]

---

64 Athalya Brenner, *The Israelite Women: Social Role in Literary Type in Biblical Narrative* (Sheffield: JSOT Press, 1985), 38-55.

65 Fiorenza, *Bread Not Stone*, 19-20.

66 Clifford, *Introducing Feminist Theology*, 65.

67 Fiorenza, *Wisdom Ways*, 183.

68 *Ibid.*, 20-21.

Summary

Consequently, we see that the Bible and its interpretations involve a complex process. Feminist hermeneutics came our as a result of the patriarchal ideology which the Bible and its interpretation reflects. Therefore, feminist hermeneutics studies the biblical text and its contexts in highlighting the prejudice embedded in the biblical text itself and also its environment. Feminist hermeneutics throughout history has developed and widened its approaches as they discover new ways of looking at and studying the text for women's liberation, and also the liberation for the oppressed. Although, various feminist scholars differ in their approaches, their essence of interpretation is the same, which is its ultimate aim, is to make the Bible a tool that can liberate and assist women to have equal status and meaningful participation in the human community. Feminist hermeneutics begin by looking at the text critically so that at the end of the process, a positive and creative interpretation can be constructed that empowers women. Thus, feminist hermeneutics is important because of its essence lies in principles of equality and justice, which are important values in christian teachings. This hermeneutics is also indispensable since it prompts other traditional interpretation to examine itself critically, thus opening new ways of creatively making sense of the biblical text in the present world and its needs.

Having highlighted the various approaches to feminist reading of the Bible, the methodology of feminist hermeneutics will be utilised in this thesis to attempt to re-read the Book of Esther in order to bring forward new images of Esther and Vashti.[69]

---

69 This thesis has not gone into a detailed study as to how the term and movement of feminism developed, because its main concern is to use feminist hermeneutics in its construction of the hidden identity of women in the Book of Esther. Therefore, the aspect of the development of the term and the movements in general are given only in brief. Also feminist hermeneutics is also varied in nature, this thesis reflects upon only those hermeneutical approaches, which will be used later in this thesis.

Chapter 2

The Historical, Political, and Social Background of the Book of Esther

In re-reading the Book of Esther it is important to know about the book, and the key issues involved in shaping the book. Therefore, in this chapter, keeping in mind of how power and authority played a dominant role in shaping the Book of Esther, the background of the book will be looked at.

2.1. Introduction: The Book of Esther

In the Talmud the book is called as Megillat Esther, or the roll of Esther. 'The Roll,' indicates a peculiar respect with which a book was held. The Hebrew Bible and Septuagint version simply calls 'Esther.' In Syriac and Vulgate the title is 'Book of Esther.' In the Hebrew Bible this book appears as the last of the five rolls, all of which are in the third 'canon' of the Old Testament, the *Ketubim* (writings). The right of Esther to a place in the canon was contested by many leading Jews and Christians down to the fourth century. Regardless of its absence at Qumran, Esther belongs to the Old Testament. The book is held to offer a paradigm for Jewish life in the Diaspora.[1]

Esther is a book about an empire ruled by absolute power, where imperial laws are irreversible. It projects the king as the personification of that absolute power, and the ruling class around him deals with those who dare to disobey. In its main plot the book narrates the anti-Jewish pogrom ordained and sanctioned by the state. But by then the Persian Empire is already in a state in which executive power is established by way of subjugating a whole 'class' of society. It is interesting to note that, the absolute power in the Persian empire of this brilliant novella is established as a response to the disobedience of one individual.[2]

The book presents three distinct voices that warrant disobedience, three timeless voices of patriarchy with which one should not comply: those that are abusive and humiliating, those motivated by fear of widespread in subordination, and those that work to eliminate all who challenge authority.[3]

2.1.1. *Date*

Various arguments have been put forward regarding the date of the book. Most probably the book was written in the Persian period, not far from the time of Artaxerxes mnemon (404-358 B.C.), by a Susian Jew, who was perfectly familiar with the palace, with Persian history, and with Persian institutions and customs. His purpose was to preserve for his people the origin and significance of Purim.

Apart from the reference to the festival of Purim in the book itself, and another in 2 Maccabees 15:36, we find no earlier reference

---

1 Sidnie. A. White, "'Esther': A Feminine Model for Jewish Diaspora," *Gender and Difference in Ancient Israel,* ed. P. L. Day (Minneapolis: Fortress Press, 1989), 161-177.

2 Bea Wyler, "Esther: The Incomplete Emancipation of Queen," *A Feminist Companion Esther, Judith and Susanna*, ed. Athalya Brenner (Sheffield: Sheffield Academic Press, 1995), 115.

3 Karol Jackowski, "Holy Disobedience in Esther," *Theology Today* XLV, no. 4 (Jan. 1989), 407.

to Purim.[4] It is viable that the choice of the 13th of Adar[5] as the day of massacre and the 14th and 15th as the days of Purim festival was deliberately made so that the first should coincide with Nicanors day, the day on which Nicanor fell in battle before Judas in 161 BCE. Thus, sometime between 160 and 100 BCE seems to be indicated for the time of writing.[6] Among the long list of Israel's nobles the name of Esther and Mordecai are lacking, almost certainly because the Book of Esther had not been written earlier than this.[7]

A close possible definition of the latest possible date may perhaps be made on the basis of the statement in 11:1 of the additions to the Book of Esther, that the book had already been translated into Greek by Lysimachus by the 4th year of Ptolemy and Cleopatra.[8] Virtually all scholars agree that the final edition took shape sometime in the 2nd century BCE, but great uncertainty surrounds the oldest date for the book's composition. It is more likely that Esther reached its final form either in the late Persian or early Hellenistic period, but in any case long before Daniel formed its final form.[9] Modern critics are unanimous in believing that the book is the product of the Greek

---

4 Scholars explain it as Babylonian New Year feast or a Persian celebration honouring the dead.

5 A later name of the twelfth month of the Jewish year borrowed by the Jews from the Babylonian calendar during the exile. It extended from the new moon of February to that of March (Esth 3:7,13; 9:15). Cf. Merrill F. Unger, "Adar," *Ungers Bible Dictionary*, ed., Merrill F. Unger (Chicago: Moody Press, 1960), 20.

6 H. Brockington, *Ezra, Nehemiah, Esther* (London: Thomas Nelson & Sons Limited, 1969), 218.

7 Davis T. Witton, ed., *Ezra, Nehemiah, Esther*: *The Century Bible* (Edinburgh: TC & EC Jack. n.y), 300.

8 H. Brockington's *Ezra, Nehemiah, Esther,* 218. This shows that the Book of Esther was in circulation by the end of 2nd century BCE if not earlier. In fixing the date for Esther's composition one must distinguish between its first and final versions. While 400 to 114 BCE seems to be the extreme limits for the first and final editions of Esther Cf. Carey A Moore, "Esther, book of," *ABD* Vol. II (New York: Doubleday & Company, 1992), 5.

9 *Ibid.,* 59.

period. The only dispute is whether it belongs to the earlier or the later part of the period.[10]

2.1.2. *Purpose*

The purpose of the Book of Esther is to demonstrate to the Jews living in Exile that it is possible to achieve success in the exile without giving up one's identity as a Jew. The book is similar to David or Tobit or Nehemiah. However, the Book of Esther is unique in respect because the protagonist of the book is a woman, Esther, who serves an important function in the story.

The purpose is to explain and justify the celebration of the festival for which there is no basis in the law by appealing to 'history' to furnish the reason for its origin and institution. The author's purpose was to reconcile divergent customs in the celebration of the festival, and to legalise the observation of 'Purim' on the Jewish calendar.[11] The second purpose is to demonstrate God's providential care of His people even to those outside Israel.[12]

2.1.3. *Authorship*

It is difficult to come to a conclusion regarding the authorship of the Book of Esther from the evidences available in the book. Different theories are available regarding its authorship. According to Donald Guthrie, it was Mordecai who wrote the Book and is supported by many ancient and modern commentators.[13] But if the Maccabean dating is followed the writer may have been a Palestinian Jew, who

---

10 Lewis Bayles Paton, *A Critical and Exegetical Commentary on the Book of Esther* (Edinburgh: T & T Clark, 1908), 6.

11 Bernhard W. Anderson, "The Book of Esther," *The Interpreters Bible* Vol. *3*, ed. Nolan B. Halman (Nashville: Abingdon Press, 1954), 824-25.

12 Mervin Breneman, "Esther," *The New American Commentary: Ezra, Nehemiah and Esther,* Vol.10, ed. E. Ray Elendenen (Nashville: Broadman & Holman Publishers, 1993), 303. His emphasis was on plot and action, not character or personality. Thus more often he simply states what was said or done, without saying why or how. Cf. Moore, "Esther, book of," 53.

13 Donald, Guthrie, *New Bible Dictionary* (Secunderabad: OM Books 1962), 350.

resided in or near Jerusalem, and who acquired his acquaintance with Persian customs and architecture through archaeological learning or extensive travelling in the east.[14] On the basis of Persian dating, the writer was probably a Persian Jew who lived in Susa or thereabouts, shortly before the final overthrow of the empire.[15] The writer of the Book of Esther provides no indications of authorship. Granted the validity of the redactional history of the book there appears to be two authors involved, the author of the original story, which was probably close to the present form of the proto-AT (Alpha Text), and the author –redactor of the MT (Massoretic Text) version.

2.1.4. *Canonicity*

The book was slow to gain acceptance as canonical, both Jewish and Christian authorities being somewhat shy of granting it the same recognition as other books in the Old Testament. Esther and her book have suffered much at the hands of interpreters through the centuries. Although very popular among the Jewish people, it was one of the last books to be accepted into the Canon, and was accepted only because of its connection with the festival of Purim. The book has been taken to task for irreligiosity, since God is not mentioned, and the only Jewish religious practice referred here is fasting (4:16).

The rabbis were troubled by Esther's failure to live as a Jew: she has several intercourses with, and marries a Gentile, lives in the Persian court, and does not follow Jewish dietary laws. In addition, Esther has been taken to task by both female and male commentators for her apparent willingness to participate in Persian harem customs, and by Christian commentators for her evident bloodthirstiness in destroying Gentiles. All this criticism however failed to grasp the true purpose of the book. Esther is the only Old Testament book not represented among the Dead Sea scrolls. Evidently the Book of Esther was not regarded as canonical by the Essene community at

14 Bernhard W. Anderson, "The Book of Esther," *The Interpreters Bible,* Vol. 3, 828.

15 *Ibid.,* 828.

Qumran,[16] though included in the canon in the council of Jamnia in AD 90. The case of opposition to the Book of Esther continued even after Jamnia. According to Brockington, a Jewish Rabbi named Samuel in the 3rd century AD was of the opinion that Esther was not a sacred book, and it did not appear in the lists of the canon made towards the end of 4th century.[17] Whatever the reason may be, it is clear that neither Levi nor Huna believed that the scroll defiled the hands.[18] The book underwent considerable hesitation due to the lack of religious elements in the story.[19] Despite its failure to mention God even once the book still has its place into the canon by popular acclaim.

If the Jews could not be unanimous about the canonical status of Esther at first neither could the christians. According to Carey A. Moore, Esther was nearly always canonical in the west, while in the east very often it was not.[20] In the Eastern Church its canonicity was a matter of dispute even in the Middle Ages, for it was stoutly denied by Nicephorus Callistus.[21] Amphilochius, Bishop of Iconium observed that only some accepted it. Even among those fathers who accepted the book as canonical, still occupied an unstable position, being listed as the last book of the canon on the list of origin.[22] Clement of Rome alluded Judith and Esther as examples of brave and godly woman in the first epistle of Clement, but whether this necessarily implies canonicity is uncertain. In any case by the 4th century the western church clearly regarded Esther as canonical through its acceptance by the council of Carthage in AD 397.[23]

---

16 Moore, "Esther, Book of," 21.

17 Brockington, *Ezra, Nehemiah, Esther*, 221.

18 Moore, "Esther, Book of," 25.

19 *Demetrius Dumm, "Tobit, Judith, Esther," New Jerome Biblical Commentary,* ed. Raymond E. Brown, Joseph Fitzmyer Murphy, Roland E. O'Carm (Bangalore: TPI, 1999), 576.

20 Moore, "Esther, Book of," 25.

21 Davies T. Witton, ed., *Ezra, Nehemiah, Esther: The Century Bible*, 292.

22 Moore, "Esther, Book of," 25.

23 Witton, *Ezra, Nehemiah, Esther: The Century Bible*, 292.

Though the views on this book has been different, generally modern scholars have accepted this book as part of the holy scripture because of its association with the festival of Purim, which is an important festival for the Jews. This was the dominant idea, which was more important than its depiction of women as having leading roles.

2.2. Background of the Book

2.2.1. *Historical Background*

The Persian Empire reached its peak in organization and power under Darius I. Darius suppressed the rebels of his empire and he organized his territory by dividing it into provinces under a governor, a commander in chief and a secretary who were directly responsible to the king. Members of the royal family were usually appointed to the important satrapies. Through these regulations the king was able to wield absolute authority over the empire.[24]

Ahasuerus the Persian king who plays a prominent part in Esther is described as a rather frivolous monarch, given to impulsive action and the issuing of sweeping laws and dependent upon the advice of the counselors and favourites.[25] He began his reign by building up

24 A. T. Olmstead, *History of the Persian Empire* (Chicago: Chicago Press, 1966), 230.

25 Various attempts have been made to identify Ahasuerus with one or another of the Persian Monarchs. The oldest identification is that with Artaxerexes, made by LXX, without indicating, which one of the three monarchs of that name may be the one, the view most generally expressed is that Ahasuerus is Xerxes (485-465 BCE). Since the Hebrew term is closest to that monarch's Persian name, Kshayarsha. On the other hand Josephus, the Targum, the Midrash, and the later commentators identify him as Artaxerxes 1 (465-425 BCE) Xerxes is a Greek derivation from the Persian Kshayarsha. Ahasuerus also refers to Xerxes 1 who reigned from 485 to 465 BC. from his father Darius 1 he inherited the great Persian Empire that extended from India to Euthopia. Xerxes himself said he was king over many tribes, among the nations he listed as 'the Indus land.' India here refers to the area drained by the Indus river, now Pakistan. Euthopia was the territory south of Egypt, now the northern part of the Sudan. This was the largest empire known up to that time. The existence of large empires and the desire for (the abuse of) power have been a part of fellow humanity's life

an army for a campaign in Egypt, which had revolted in the lifetime of Darius. He acted with great severity, forcing the Egyptians to nurse their hatred in secret while awaiting their revenge.[26] Before his expedition against Greece, Ahasuerus had to suppress a revolt in Babylonia[27] because two rebels had assumed power and had tablets dated by their names.[28] The war with Greece struggled on, while Ahasuerus lost his energy since he was a victim of his harem, which seems to have been a dominating interest of his life.[29] He also carried on an expedition again at Greece, which was well organized and shrewdly prepared since he had adherents and friends in many Greek states.[30] After his defeat in Greece Ahasuerus devoted himself to the building of Persepolisand to the harem.[31] After the defeats in

---

on earth during the greater part of history (Gen.11). The 127 provinces in the Book of Esther are thought by some to be inaccurate since Herodotus listed thirty Satrapies. The term 'province' however refers to a subdivision of a satrapy (Ezra 2:1) and their number varied (Dan: 6:1). Cf. *Ibid.*, 231-34.

26 R. Ghrishman , *Iran* (Suffolk: Richard Clay & Company Ltd., 1954), 191.

27 He acted with the same brutality towards the Babylonian after which he ceased to use the title of 'King of Babylon' calling himself 'king of Persian and Medes,' hence placing the royal confidence only on the ruling people. Cf. *Ibid.*, 191.

28 Megabyzus a general of the King crushed the revolt and punished the Babylonian severely. They demolished its fortification, destroyed the temple and melted the Golden Statue of Marduk and estates were confisticated and given to the Persians. Cf. Geo Widengren, "The Persians," *Peoples of Old Testament Times,* ed., D. J. Wiseman (Oxford: Clarendon Press, 1973), 326-327.

29 *Ibid.,* 326-327.

30 *Ibid.,* 327. The invasion against the Greeks was not an object of his thought but it was his cousin Mardonius who was the son of Gobryas and Darius's sister who had more influence with Ahasuerus than anyone else in the kingdom influenced him to punish the Athenians who had harmed them. Cf. Herodotus, *The Histories,* trans. Aubrey de Selincourt (Suffolk: Penguin Books Ltd, 1954), 414.

31 Richard N. Faye, *The Heritage of Persia* (New York: Mentor Books, 1966), 149.

Greece in 464 B.C., Ahasuerus was assassinated and his third son Artaxerxes 1 (Longimanus) succeeded him.[32]

2.2.2. *Political Background*

Ahasuerus Empire was governed strictly according to the imperial law. Once issued, in fact, the king's law could not be rescinded. Ahasuerus followed a less tolerant policy towards his subjects than his father. When he conquered Egypt he dealt with them in a harsher manner than his predecessor. The Persians rule over the Egyptians were different from that of Pharaohs. They did not respect their native customs nor their religious practices. The Persians further treated the Babylonians with contempt. Toward the end of his reign, Ahasuerus was no longer interested in visiting the troops in battle and ignored the doings of his generals. Instead he gave more of his time to the numerous harem intrigues. He began the practice of monogamy as was practiced by the later Persian kings. He married only one woman but maintained a harem of 360 concubines from the provinces.[33]

2.2.3. *Social Background*

Sociologically, it is no secret that men were seen distinctly as the master of their house in particular and of society in general, not only at a period of history during which the story might have taken place, but also throughout all recorded Jewish history, where men were the leaders, the scholars, the rabbis, the authorities. Women tended to the home and children/family. In this sense Ahasuerus can be seen not only as an ultimate authority that holds vast power over everyone, but also more generally as a male, patriarchal authority in relation to females.[34]

32 Charles Foster Kent, *A History of Jewish People* (London: Smith, Elder & Co, 1912), 155.

33 Faye, *The Heritage of Persia*, 149.

34 Mary Gendler, as quoted by Diana Lipton, "The Woman's Lot in Esther," *Bodies, Lives, Voices: Gender in Theology*, eds., Kathleen O' Grady et al. (Sheffield: Sheffield Academic Press 1998), 135-136.

The Medo-Persiunas are the master race and the Persian administration has inherited from its Neo-Babylonian predecessor's potentially disaffected members of an exiled people. It is a world where the wish of the King instantly attains the status of law and where the king's wish is often his whims (1.12; 2.1). It is a world ruled by law and regulation in which serving of wine is the subject of royal edict (1.8), The bedfellows of the king were determined by a complex administrative machinery (2.12-14) and the authority of everyman's house in the empire was regulated by a multilingual decree (1.20,22).[35]

2.2.4. *Portrayal of Ahasuerus*

Traditionally Ahasuerus[36] (486-465) is remembered as a weak monarch dominated by his eunuchs and for his insane attack on European Greece. He was 35 years when he succeeded his father, before which, he was trained as successor by acting as viceroy of Babylon. His reign is significant for the administrative changes.[37]

Ahasuerus was an ambitious, ruthless, intolerant ruler and administrator over a vast empire, a brilliant warrior and a jealous

35 David J. A. Clines, *The Esther Scroll: The Story of the Story* (Sheffield: University of Sheffield, 1984), 10-11.

36 Shortly after Ahasuerus accession he razes a portion of Darius' treasury at Persepolis to build the harem. He was not the eldest son, the eldest son of Darius was Artobazanes who was already recognize as the successor by 507(Babylonian document), but his mother was a commoner unnamed daughter of Gobryas. But Ahasuerus was born to Atossa daughter of the empire's founder, when a bitter quarrel arose regarding the succession Ahasuerus was chosen as a son born of high woman. His brother Ariamenes set forth to contest the throne but won over by gifts and promise that he would make him loyal till his death. Cf. Olmstead, *History of the Persian Empire*, 214-215, 231-232.
According to Herodotus Demaratus was the Spartan king, which had been deposed and had gone for voluntary exile. The story goes that when he heard of the dispute he went to Ahasuerus and had advised him to point out that Artobazanes was born before his father held any public office and that Darius was on the throne when he was born. Cf. Herodotus, *The Histories,* 414.

37 Olmstead, *History of the Persian Empire*, 230.

lover.[38] His greatest achievement was the completion of the palace complex Darius began, a marvel of grandeur, beauty and luxury.[39] For nearly three years his word had been law to millions of men and women: and all the richest countries, far and near, had laid their treasures at his feet.

According to Mildred Duff and Noel Hope,

> It is terrible to think of one man possessing such unlimited power; his subjects bowed before him with the trembling reverence that should only be given to God. They crawled into his presence on their knees: they pretended that the sight of his awful majesty dazzled their eyes which made him proud to think that no king ever lived than to compare with himself for splendour and wisdom.[40]

Ahasuerus was said to have treated his people cruelly. Herodotus recounts quite a few bizarre episodes that have to do with his wives and concubines. C.E. Van states that the first signs of decay in the Persian empire appeared during Ahasuerus' reign. Ahasuerus was weak, possessing a tyrannical character and loved luxury as expected of a prince reared at court.[41] Herodotus confirmed Ahasuerus claims

38 David M. Howard, "Esther, Theology of," *The New International Dictionary of Old Testament Theology and Exegesis,* Vol. 4, ed. Willem A. Van Gimeren (Nashville: Paternoster Press, 1997), 582.

39 A foundation stone contained the following inscription "I am Xerxes, the great king. The only king, the king of all countries which speak all kinds of languages, the king of this entire big and far reaching earth, the son of King Darius, the Achaemenian, a Persian, a son of a Persian, an army of Aryan descent" So thought king Ahasuerus as "he sat on the throne of his kingdom, which was in Shushan, the palace"(Esther 1:2) and he lifted his proud head higher, and looked haughtily down at the princes and nobles who sat beneath him, and knew himself to be the richest and mightiest ruler of the widest empire the world had ever known. Cf. Mildred Duff and Noel Hope, *Esther, the Queen, on Life in the Ancient Palace of Shushan* (London, Edinburgh & New York: Marshall Brothers, Ltd, n.y), 5.

40 *Ibid.*, 6.

41 C. E. Van Sickle, *A Political and Cultural History of Ancient World* (Boston: Houghton Wifflin, 1947), 151.

of extensive political power. On the other hand, Ahasuerus did not measure up to the moral qualities of his predecessors.[42]

The rabbis under the Parthians who were direct successors of the Persians, carefully portray the Persian Kings so as not to offend their hosts by making derogatory comments. The rabbis in acknowledging the might of King Ahasuerus depicts him as one of the only three kings who ruled over the entire earth, but presenting a negative picture where at the banquet for his subjects, Ahasuerus, actually had regard for the Jews 'dietary laws' and their rule forbidding drinking of wine that had been touched by a non Jew, gives. Some rabbis expressed that Ahasuerus was unfit to be the king, but raised himself to that position by virtue of his wealth.[43]

Ahasuerus was definitely less capable than his father, who was one of history's great rulers. He was neither a statesman nor a general and lacked the magnanimity of his father.[44] Ahasuerus also had some significant military and artistic accomplishments, though the Greek expedition failed, but he reconquered Egypt and suppressed an important rebellion in Babylon. In this process he further strengthened the powerful military force Darius had built up.[45] According G. Riccioth, "he inherited none of the good qualities of his predecessors but only a love of opulent display, which progressively shaped his moral fiber."[46]

---

42 G. Ricciotti, *The History of Israel*, Vol. 2 (Milwaukee: Bruce, 1955), 16.

43 Ahasuerus is referred as wicked, and an anonymous comment on the very first verse in the Book of Esther, the word wh (he) indicates that he persisted in his wickedness from bringing to end. Ahasuerus in his greed is compared to "a ravenous bear" in Prov. 28:15. He is also depicted as a drunkard, moreover, the rabbis stress Ahasuerus' immorality, noting that he ordered that force be used in taking maidens away from their parents and wives from their husbands in acquiring them from his harem. Cf. Louis H. Feldman, " 'Josephus' Portrait of Ahasuerus," *Australian Biblical Review,* XL11(1994): 27-28.

44 Widengren "The Persians," *Peoples of Old Testament Times*, 327.

45 Brenemen, *The New American Bible Commentary: Ezra, Nehemiah and Esther*, 278.

46 Ricciotti, *The History of Israel*, 16.

Summary

The historical, social and political background behind the Book of Esther shows us how patriarchal power has been the dominant motive in the reign of the king and his men. Thus, such settings motivated the writer to write the book, by imposing the roles that Esther and Vashti had to play in a male dominated society. In this environment, the king enjoyed absolute power, which became the main domain in shaping the Book of Esther and its characters. The law of the king decides everything and if his wishes were not considered, then one is put into a position of slave or a concubine. Under the king there were probably people who were the noble class and who held positions given by the king for his advantage. Therefore, the background of the time of Esther depicts that people were restricted by patriarchal and hierarchal powers. Where those in power and authority had all the privilege and responsibility, which often resulted in misuse of power by those in authority. The people who were usually the subjects of such kings were in his mercy. Their lives existed to pleasure the king and to obey the king or those persons in authority. Thus, we clearly see a time where there is domination by those in power and oppression of those without power.

Chapter 3

The Search for the Hidden Identity of Vashti and Esther
An Exegetical Study

Before probing into the identity of Esther and Vashti, the identity of women in Ancient Israel, the Jewish and Persian community will be taken into consideration.

3.1. Identity of Women

3.1.1. *Identity of Women in Ancient Israel*

Women's identity in ancient Israel comes from the laws and stories in the Hebrew Bible. The basic unit in the Hebrew society was the family, headed by the father; called as "the father's house." Women were identified as child bearer for her husband. Adultery by a married woman was punishable by death, whereas the infidelity by the husband was not considered a crime, unless it was with a married woman. Brides were supposed to be virgins, and those committing fornication were executed. Divorce was practiced, but only as a male prerogative. Women did not have the rights to property.[1] A woman was always under the authority of some man: first her father and then her husband, which is perhaps the key to the way in which the Israelite women were treated.

Only men were qualified to become priests and attend the three annual pilgrim feasts. Women were restricted from holding such offices and participating in feasts because of ritual uncleanliness from menstruation and childbirth. Thus according to Bird,

> The picture of woman obtained from the Old Testament Laws is seen as someone invisible, inferior, in a male-centred and male-dominated society. The laws, by and large, do not address her; most do not even acknowledge her existence. She comes to view only in situations where males are lacking in essential socio-economic roles, where she requires special protection, where sexual offences involving women are treated and were sexually defined or sexually differentiated states, roles and/or occupations are dealt with. Where ranking occurs she is always honoured as equivalent to man. Nevertheless, she is always subject to the authority of some male, except when widowed or divorced-an existentially precarious of independence in Israel.[2]

C. J. Vos points out that, there are no rules for delineating the subordination of the wives, nowhere is the wife told to honour or obey her husband, there are also no regulations for dealing with the disobedient wife as there are for children.[3] The patriarchal structure of society and in particular the family was not justified by a doctrinal theory, nor by the law, but rather it was simply taken for granted,

1 Alice Ogden Bellis, *Helpmates, Harlots, Heroes: Women's Stories in the Hebrew Bible* (Louisville: Westminster John Knox Press, 1994), 21.

2 Phyllis A. Bird, "Images of Women in the Old Testament," in *Religion and Sexism: Images of Woman in the Jewish and Christian Tradition,* ed., Rosemary Radford Ruether (New York: Simon & Schuster, 1974), 41-88.

3 C. J. Vos, *Women in the Old Testament Worship* (Delhi: Judels and Brinkman, 1968), 46.

based on the certainty that the soul of man is the stronger.[4] J. L. McKenzie points out that women in Israel, like children and slaves, could not make moral decisions.[5] Their oaths had to be ratified by husband or father before they could become valid, for the women did not have the freedom of moral responsibility. Thus, we have a picture of the Israelite women, subordinate to their husbands, and generally enjoying a lower status than men.

3.1.2. *Identity of Women in the Jewish Community*

The Jewish tradition is rich in sayings, which reflect the subordinate position of women. The structure of the synagogue, and the Jewish society is masculine. From the rites of circumcision to the burial rites only men are understood as an Israelite, one who could study the Torah.[6] Laws in the Old Testament were directed at men. Women could not receive the sign of membership in the religious community (Gen. 17:10ff). Priesthood was reserved only for men. Women were allowed in the Gentiles court but with restriction.[7]

Each Jewish community in Palestine and throughout the Diaspora usually had at least one synagogue, an institution of prayer and study of law; its origins go back to the time of Ezra and possibly to the exile. At the time of the Roman Emperor Augustus he had two separate areas: The *Sabbateion* for worship services and the *andron* for lectures on and discussion of the law by the scribes and their

4 J. Pedersen, *Israel: Its Life and Culture* (London: Oxford University Press, 1926), 76.

5 Property was passed from father to son. Only when no sons were available could daughters inherit, but they were required to marry their clan. As a result, the property would remain within their clan, where their sons eventually inherit the property. Cf. J. L. McKenzie, *A Theology of the Old Testament* (New York: Chapman, 1974), 228.

6 Kristen Stendahl, *The Bible and the Role of Women*, Trans. Emilie T. Sander (Philadelphia: Fortress Press, 1966), 27.

7 Before time the court of women was free of buildings, and they surround it with a gallery so that the women should observe from above, the men from below and that they should not mingle together. Cf. Herbert Danby, "Middoth 2, 5," *The Mishnah* (Oxford: Clarendon Press, 1933), 592.

students. The latter room was exclusively for males. Even in the prayer hall some sort of barriers separated the sexes.[8] Discrimination is seen in their famous prayer, which was recited in the synagogue.[9]

A predominance of the concept of male participation in the worship played the most prominent role in most of the cultic acts. The religious community was made up of adult males, circumcised as the sign of the covenant. According to Walter Eichrodt, "it is a covenant with those who are competent to enter into such a thing: that is to say with the men; they represent the people...woman has no place in this revelation, therefore, she is a constant danger to the worship of Yahweh."[10] However, according to him the congregation of Yahweh includes the family where neither age nor sex bestow any special privilege.

Women did not receive circumcision, an outward sign of the covenant, which symbolically expresses the fact that women were of secondary status by birth, 'second class citizens'.[11] In spite of not undergoing the rite of circumcision they were never seen as part of the despised and detested 'uncircumcised' but it reflects their lower status in the society. The Israelite woman was responsible equally with the man for keeping the law and maintaining the purity of the culture. The law was read aloud to both men and women and if they did not seek the Lord with their whole heart and transgress the law both of them would be put to death.[12]

As the representatives of their household sacrifices were brought by men. Leviticus 12:6 and 15:29 show that women were expected to take an independent role in bringing sacrifices. According to C.J. Vos

---

8 Leonard Swindler, *Biblical Affirmation of Woman* (Philadelphia: The Westminster Press, 1979), 147.

9 "Blessed art thou, O Lord our God, who has not made me a woman," cited by Everett Ferguson, *Backgrounds of Early Christianity* (Grand Rapids, MI: William B. Eerdmans Publishing Company, 1993), 71.

10 W. Eichrodt, *Theology of the Old Testament* (London: SCM Press Ltd., 1961), 131.

11 Mary J. Evans, *Woman in the Bible* (Carlisle, UK: Paternoster Press, 1983), 27.

12 2 Chronicles15: 12-13; Deuteronomy 17:2-5; 29:18-21.

"whenever a sacrifice was required of an individual, no evidence has been found which would cause us to doubt that if that individual was a woman she was expected to fulfil personally this requirement."[13]

All Israelite males were required by the law to 'appear before the Lord' three times a year at the major feasts.[14] Women were not under any such obligation. There was no reason as to this though it seems likely that their responsibilities at home and their frequent ritual uncleanness may be the reason. Women were presentable along with men to come before God, which was possible when they came under the authority of their husbands. They were seen as enquiring God through the prophets directly and independently. The husband or father had power of canceling the vows of woman. If they were not so canceled, then the woman was as responsible as man for fulfilling the vow.[15]

3.1.3. *Identity of Women in the Persian Community*

Women in the world of the Persian Diaspora were essentially powerless and marginalized members of society. Even if they belonged to the dominant culture, they could not grasp power, as a man could. Whatever power they could attained was through the manipulation of men, the holders of power. In this sense the exiled Jew could identify with the woman as marginalized person, where power could be obtained only through one's wits and talents.[16] Women were under

13 Vos, *Women in the Old Testament Worship*,130.

14 Exodus 23:17; 34:23, Deuteronomy 16:16.

15 The cases of Rebecca in Genesis 22:22, and Jeroboam's wife, 1Kings 14:1 & Hagar in Genesis 16:17.

16 By astutely using her beauty, charm and political intelligence, and by taking one well-placed risk, Esther saves her people, brings about the downfall of their enemy, and elevates her kinsman to the highest position in the kingdom. The second unique aspect of the Hebrew Book of Esther is the absence of any overt religious element. Many commentators have argued that religious beliefs, such as a belief in God's protection of the chosen people are present (4:14). This argument may be valid: However, it remains true that the presence of God is conspicuously absent. Jewish identity seems to be primarily ethic not religious. It is when Esther is that makes her Jewish, rather than what

the control of men, and they scoffed at those who were bold, direct, aggressive and disobedient. The exemplary women were those who were unassuming, quietly persistent and who gained power through the love they inspired in men. These women lived almost vicariously, subordinating their needs and desires to those of others.[17]

3.2. Exegetical Study of Selected Texts

Observing that the patriarchal structure had shaped the identity of women in the Israelite, Jewish and Persian community, this section aims to view the hidden identity of Vashti and Esther by using the different feminist hermeneutical approaches in re-reading the two identities.

The stories of Vashti and Esther received significant reinterpretation in the light of contemporary concern over the status of women in church and society. Vashti in later Judeo-Christian tradition was despised for her disobedience to her husband, though she shows remarkable courage in refusing to demean herself before some drunken men.[18] According to Elisabeth Moltmann–Wendel, though figures of contrasts like Vashti, the first wife of king Ahasuerus who rejected men, were replaced by Esther, disappeared from view in the Bible it must be recovered through our own history.[19]

---

she practices or believes. This indicates that the audience for the book was primarily in the Diaspora, where certain religious practices, such as worship in the temple, were simply not possible, and Jewish ethnic identity was in danger of disappearing in the great melting pot of the ancient Near East. Cf. Sidnie White Crawford, "Esther," in *Women in Scripture: A Dictionary of Named and Unnamed Women in the Hebrew Bible, the Apocryphal/Deuterocanonical Books and the New Testament*, ed., Carol Meyers et al. (New York: Houghton Wifflin Company, 2000), 75-77.

17 Mary Gendler, as quoted by Diana Lipton, "The Woman's Lot in Esther," *Bodies, Lives, Voices: Gender in Theology*, ed. Kathleen O'Grady et al. (Sheffield: Sheffield Academic Press 1998), 135-136.

18 Barbara J. Machaffie, *Her Story: Women in Christian Tradition* (London: A & C Black, 1986), 10.

19 Elisabeth Moltmann-Wendell, *A Land Flowing with Milk and Honey: Perspectives on Feminist Theology* (New York: Crossroad, 1986), 198.

This chapter attempts to carry out the Exegetical study of Chapter 1 and 2, which portrays the patriarchal power. Both the section on Vashti and Esther will be dealt with separately. The context where the identity of Woman was formulated must be kept in mind as we attempt to do the exegetical study. The writer explores only those texts of the Book of Esther, which portray the identity of Esther and Vashti as mere objects.

3.2.1. *Exegetical Study of Esther 1:1-23*

The opening verses of the book describe a one hundred and eighty day feast given by the king in the third year (484 B.C.) of his reign. His guest were princes and nobles from all realm who came for a successive relays for a period of six months to enjoy the king's favour and to be impressed by the king's court and to admire the majesty of his imperial person. The motive of the banquet was to exhibit the king's wealth and power, but it ended with ironic consequences.[20] The Persians had an insatiate passion for banqueting. At the close of this series of banquets where another expedition to Greece was decided a banquet of seven days was given to the citizens of Susa.[21]

3.2.1.1. *The King's Honour and Power* (Vv. 1-10)

Here the display and demand sections are linked by the language and motif. The display (בהראת) of his riches in the first section is mirrored by the display (להראות) of Vashti at the beginning of the second section along with the second banquet's guest list (v. 5) which is mirrored by the ranking and totality of those affected by Vashti's wrong (v. 16) and by the king's new law (v. 20). The *yeqar* (יקר) in v. 4 is also the יקר which every man must enjoy in his own home in v. 20. In Vashti's account the concern with status as a symbolic sphere is precise. The use of Hiphil infinitive construct with ראה parallels the

20 Merwin Breneman, "Esther," in *The New American Commentary: Ezra, Nehemiah and Esther*, Vol. 10. ed. E. Ray Elendenen (Nashville: Broadman & Holman Publishers, 1993), 307.

21 Ira Maurice Price, Ovid R. Selles & E. Leslie Carlson, *The Monuments and the Old Testament* (Philadelphia: The Judson Press, 1958), 337.

king's intention to 'show off' the glory of his wealth in v.4 and the beauty of his wife and queen in v. 11. She was meant to be on display as his greatest status symbol during the grand finale of his double celebration. The king commanded her to perform, to confirm her role as the obedient, beautiful 'pleasing' queen. The purpose of the king's banquet is clear: they are the occasions for the king to honour himself. Vashti's episode describes a complete and unexpected blow to the king's honour. Even the display of Vashti's beauty was meant to be the highest moment of the series of feasts, the final exhibition of the king's royal treasury. Her refusal effectively undermines the purpose of the half-year celebration and potentially disrupted the social order across the empire. It wasperceived by males in position of control as a global threat to their honour. She had publicly disobeyed not only as queen but also as representative wife.

The 'nobles-officials' and 'military leaders'present in the banquet indicate the elite of the army and princes who came from all over the empire, in order to see these luxuries. His feast was exclusively for the elite who were all men. This clearly indicates the importance given to men. This feast is not just majestic; it is also very male since in the following verse Queen Vashti also gave a banquet. Vashti the queen entertained the women in a separate feast of similar magnificence. Ahasuerus' excess at wine confused his brain and he ordered his chamberlains to bring in and exhibit his wife before his intoxicated guests. Herodotus tells us that Macedonian ladies introduced to a similar banquet in Darius' days were basely insulted.[22] The kingdom is so secure that all its high officials can have feasts at the king's party and then he directs his attention to the other strata of his royal dominion, namely 'all the people who were found in the acropolis of Susa, from the greatest to the least.' One might well suspect that while 'from greatest to least' covers several classes of people within the social order, it may not include women. The suspicion is confirmed in v. 9. It is assumed that the king throws this party not out of his goodness of heart but in order to secure the next strata of the social

22 Ira Maurice Price, Ovid R. Selles & E. Leslie Carlson, *The Monuments and the Old Testament* (Philadelphia: The Judson Press, 1958), 337.

order. Few references are made to the king's rule along with several other words suggesting pre-eminence or security.

The purpose of the festivals is to demonstrate the king's honour, which became the dominating theme in the book and emerges as an important means for consolidating power. In its anthropological studies, honour is closely related to social power, especially male dominance. Thus, there exist a relationship between patriarchy and socio-economic hierarchies of power. Moreover, the king's honour is related to men's honour, especially in relation to their status over women.[23]

Honour is demonstrated as a substance in 1:4. Two sets of double constructs which could be translated literally, 'the riches of the glory of the kingship and the honour of the beauty of his greatness.' A more accurate translation would be 'the riches of his glorious kingship' and 'the honour of his beautiful greatness.' Attempts have been made here to pair two different kinds of 'objects' on display. The first refers to the wealth while the second suggests splendour or beauty.[24] The description of the second feast pictures a liberal king lavishly entertaining his citizens. There was no restraint in the guests drinking; they were to drink according to their own desires (v. 8).[25]

---

23 In ancient cultures, the most specific and primary condition for achieving honour is autonomy. One of the principal determinants of honour is sexual autonomy, and in the sexual sphere only men could be autonomous. Women are marked as sexual beings by public awareness of menses and pregnancy, while men bear no outward witness of sexual activities. In such social structure only men can be fully autonomous and be worthy of honour. Other elements of masculine honour involve providing for and protecting the reflected honour of the family, social prominence, manly courage and virility. Males can demonstrate their sexuality even aggressively where as women cannot. Cf. Lillian R. Klein "Honour and Shame," in *A Feminist Companion to Esther, Judith and Susanna,* ed. Athalya Brenner (Sheffield: Sheffield Academic Press, 1995), 149-156.

24 Timothy S. Laniak, *Shame and Honour in the Book of Esther* (Georgia: Scholars Press, 1998), 45.

25 Ancient historians often comment on the abundance of wine in the Persian court. *Ibid.*, 45.

V. 9: The phrase ושתי המלכה עשתה משתה (Queen Vashti also gave a banquet) depicts that a separate banquet for the women was held in the same house. Here the word 'separate' can mean 'unequal' because the royal house where 'the women' assembled are not really theirs, but the property of king Ahasuerus.[26] It is worth noting that Persian class distinctions were evidently strictly observed, being indicated twice that the king gives two banquets first for the nobility followed by one for the masses of the people (1:5-8).[27] The main banquet excluded the presence of women because they were considered as inferior and unworthy to celebrate and share equally with the men. This dichotomy of feasts establishes an emphasis on sexuality and gender roles, which the king makes explicit when he "commanded the seven eunuchs who served King Ahasuerus as chamberlains to bring queen Vashti before the king with her royal crown in order to show the peoples and praises her beauty, for she was fair to behold."

V.10: King Ahasuerus was in high spirits, which probably indicates that he was at least partly inebriated. In Hebrew anthropology the 'heart' is the seat of the will and of thought. The expression 'good of heart' means to be in an expansive and happy mood. But when the condition is brought on by alcohol, it also implies the impairment of judgment.[28]

3.2.1.2. *Vashti's Refusal to the King* (Vv. 11-22)

V. 11: Having displayed his wealth and generosity, the King now sends the eunuchs[29] for his beautiful wife ordering her to wear the

26 Bruce W. Jones, "Two Misconceptions about the Book of Esther," *CBQ* XXXIX, no. 2 (April 1977), 173.

27 Robert Gordis, "Studies in the Esther Narrative," *JBL* 95 (1982): 46.

28 Frederic Bush, "Esther," *WBC,* Vol. 9, 349.

29 In Esther the term 'סריס' has a polysemantic range of meaning and referents, designating four kinds of Persian royal officials who were eunuchs: eunuchs incharge of the harem (Esth 2:3,14-15), eunuch attendants of the queen (4:4-5), eunuch guards of the king's private apartment (2:21; 6:2) and eunuch attendants of the king (1:10,12,15;6:14;7:9). The polysemantic nature of סרים encompasses their physical condition of eunuchs and their official position of royal attendants. Cf. Gordon H. Johnston, 'סריס' in *The New International*

royal crown. In those days the king had the advantage of searching for fair young virgins, whose only consideration was to please him. Consulting her was like consulting an animal, what mattered was her beauty.[30]

V. 12: The Hebrew text gives no reason or justification for Vashti's refusal of a direct command from the King. Josephus informs that she refused to come because Persian law forbade wives to be seen by strangers. The king known to be impulsive and cruel enough to kill anyone, who defied him or gave him advice that went against his will, became furious.[31] The text does not state whether the king intents to display Vashti in the nude, but its emphasis on Ahasuerus drunkenness when he summoned Vashti suggests that his intentions were less honourable.

Therefore, Vashti's refusal to the king was commented upon by most of the scholars that she may have known of his intent and so refused to be exhibited. Ahasuerus on consulting his chief counsellor disposed of her. During the next four years he was busily engrossed in preparing and conducting his memorable expedition against Greece. Probably necessary preparation was in the making to secure a queen for the place of Vashti the queen's refusal to come at the king's bidding marks the first and only point in the narrative where the royal impetus is brought low, just when his 187 daylong demonstrations of his honour and power are about to come to its final climax.[32] The king could have been furious because the queen did not fulfil his whims or refused to appear in the presence of the officers. The King and the officers could take this refusal as a serious offence.

Vv. 17-22: The first term, which deserves attention, is the verb usually translated, 'wronged.' Est.1:16 employs one of several

---

Dictionary of Old Testament Theology and Exegesis, Vol. 3, ed., Willem A. Van Gimeren (Nashville: Paternoster Press, 1997), 293.

30 Letha Scanzoni & Nancy Hardesty, *All we're Meant to be: A Biblical Approach to Women's Liberation* (Waco, Texas: Word Books, 1975), 93.

31 Breneman, "Esther," 308.

32 Timothy K. Beal, "Tracing Esther's Beginning," in *A Feminist Companion to Esther, Judith and Susanna*, ed. Athalya Brenner, (Sheffield: Sheffield Academic Press, 1995), 95.

denominative uses of עוה (BDB, root #2), derived from the common term for iniquity עון. Verbs with these same three radicals in Hebrew presumably represent another, distinct Semitic root which literally means, 'to bend or twist' (BDB, root #1). Often metaphorically in reference to unacceptable behaviour, this verb carries the connotations of shame. Which means that Queen Vashti had similarly 'wronged' King Ahasuerus by disgracing him at a crisis moment of royal vulnerability. Queen Vashti is depicted as the one committing the wrong because of her disobedience to the king, which was

The phrase בעניהן להבזות בעליהן literally translates, 'to despise their husbands in their eyes.' The root בזה implies value judgment in status contexts like Esther 1. The word 'despised in her heart' (ותבז לו בלבה) her husband the king as he danced among the commoners 'just like one of the commoners.' He was not worthy of respect because he did not maintain the boundaries of his position. The result was 'plenty of contempt and anger'(1:18).[33]

Confronted with a new case the king reached out for advice from his experts. Memucan, one of the court officials understood the boldness of the queen as questioning not only the King's position, but also of all the men's position, therefore he proposed that Queen Vashti be punished by making a law to banish and strip her of her royal status. Her transgression was that of a 'woman'. That she also functioned as the queen was of lesser significance. Most surprising is his repeated emphasis on Vashti's womanhood, when he ponders (v. 17) what the noble women throughout the empire would eventually use as justification for their own disobedience.

The banishing of Vashti was the first step in redressing her as wrong. The next step was the formulation of a law, which would

33 Vashti's contempt is compared to one of Israel's dishonourable priests. When Eli showed more honour for his own sons than for the sacrifices of the tent, God broke his covenant with Eli's line. The explanation given in 1 Sam 2:30 is simply a variation on the code of honour so often repeated in Mediterranean cultures today: "those who honour me I will honour; but those who despise me will be lightly esteemed." The covenant was publicly broken by God because it was already publicly broken by Eli's dishonouring and despising behaviour. Cf. Laniak, *Honour and Shame in the Book of Esther*, 54-55.

prevent the effect of her act. The purpose of the proposed edict, in v. 20 is that "all women will give honour to their husbands." Disobedience[34] was rectified by honour and the nuance of obedience is confirmed again in v. 22 where each husband is given the authoritative position of 'ruler' (שׂרר) in his own home.[35] According to George A. F. Knight, "was not everyman already a ruler in his own house in ancient Persia?"[36] So evidently the writer of the book is scoffing at the dominance of the male over the female, in a land where women were treated as chattels.

This exposed Memucan's deep concern. The noble women would hardly refer to the queen as 'Vashti' but rather as 'the queen': for him as a man, however 'Vashti' is dangerous precisely because she

34 Disobedience and obedience are established as major motifs in the book. It is about an empire ruled by absolute power, where imperial laws are irreversible. It is also about how the king who personifies that absolute power, and the ruling class around him deal with those who dare to disobey. It also narrates the anti-Jewish pogrom ordained, and sanctioned by the state. But, by then the Persian Empire is already in a state in which executive power is established by way of subjugating a whole 'class' of society. The absolute power in the Persian Empire is established as a response to the disobedience of one individual.

35 This proposal reflects an analogical relationship among various social slots. For example, children respect their parents, their wives, and their husbands. Fathers act honourably over their families as chiefs do over tribes or as elders over kin-groups. Kings become the archetypal human head, and king honour functions as the archetype of father-honour or husband honour. . In Esther, the king's edict is sent out to ensure that every man will be "ruler over his own household" (v.22). In the face of an incipient revolt of the women, the king takes official measures to reassert the husbands authority. The Persians were liberal in granting cultural and religious autonomy to the various peoples living under their rule, so that even royal decrees were promulgated in various languages. When a marriage took place between people of different people of different ethnic background, the mother's language would normally prevail in the home and tend to become the language of the children. Nehemiah explicitly complains that when some Jews married foreign wives, their children spoke the language of their mothers (Neh 13:24-24) Ahasuerus' edict was designed to make the fathers language dominant in the home which shows the superiority of men."

36 G. A. F. Knight, *Esther, Song of Songs, Lamentations: Introduction and Commentary* (London: SCM Press Ltd., 1955), 29.

is a woman rather than because of her queenship.[37] Since she refuses to be degraded to the position of concubine says Bickerman,[38] Vashti should not appear before the king. The text certainly does not say that she was dead because the death penalty was reserved for those who appeared uninvited before the king and that precisely is what she did not do. Many commentators, however understand her sentence to be a death sentence. A new queen then was to be appointed, who was not like Vashti with a well-developed sense of dignity and boldness, rather someone better, for whom only obedience is part of her character.[39]

The request for Vashti's presence at the banquet is a crude form of male chauvinism, and the reaction to her refusal is even more chauvinistic, where the courtiers magnify Vashti's disobedience into a crime against every husband in the empire. Vashti refused to be men's sexual object and her husband's toy.[40]

The introduction of the new law was not because women enjoyed so much freedom earlier, but because men were afraid that other women would be encouraged by Vashti's act and challenge the authorities, which only demonstrates a deep seated sense of men's insecurity because their defence was at work in full force. Her refusal to come at the king's bidding marks the first point in the narrative where the royal power is lowered. It was probably assumed that women would get all kinds of crazy notions in their heads, even the idea that they were men's equals, capable of making their own decisions, where man no longer would be safe in his own house.[41] The message conveyed here loud and clear is that bold, direct, and

---

37 Bea Wyler, "Esther: The Incomplete Emancipation of a Queen," in *A Feminist Companion To Esther, Judith and Susanna*,ed. Athalya Brenner (Sheffield: Sheffield Academic Press, 1995), 118.

38 Elias Bickerman, *Four Strange Books of the Bible: Jonah, Daniel, Koheleth, Esther* (New York: Schocken Books, 1967), 186.

39 Wyler, "Esther: The Incomplete Emancipation of a Queen," 119.

40 Alice Laffey, *An Introduction to the Old Testament: A Feminist Perspective* (Philadelphia: Fortress Press, 1988), 216.

41 Renita J. Weems, *Just a Sister Away: A Womanist Vision of Women's Relationships in the Bible* (San Diego: Lura Media, 1988), 103.

aggressive women are not tolerable, since they threaten the power of patriarchy, rather the worthy women are those who are unassuming, quietly feeble and who gain power through the love they inspire in men.

3.3. Interpretation of the Identity of Vashti

Vashti's story is a common story that happens with women who are marginalized. No commentators mention any significant issues of translation or textual variants in the first chapter. Though Vashti as a person is always implied as representing something negative, however her Vashti's name coveys something else.[42] The structure of the entire story chiastically resolves around feasts, culminating with festival of Purim in Susa. Royalty is introduced as a common denominator of objects both as animate and inanimate, where power and rank is related with royalty. The themes of control, law and obedience are introduced as the characterization of the king who depended on his council. A sense of extravagance is seen in the numbers of provinces, guests and days. Elements of both tragedy and comedy are seen especially during Vashti episode.[43]

The opening verse that reads, "in the days of Ahasuerus who reigned over 127 provinces from India to Ethiopia…" is a statement about universal sovereignty.[44] The static description of the kingdom,

---

42 The name 'Vashti' which comes from the Persian word Vashista ('best'), is unattested in extra biblical sources.' Most likely, Vashti is not a proper name, as most kings in the Ancient Near East had more than one wife, and Persian rulers were often noted for having harems, it is likely that Vashti was the 'best' or 'first' wife: she is called queen in the text, which is an honour usually reserved for the first wife. Cf. Lewis Bayles Paton, *A Critical and Exegetical Commentary on the Book of Esther,* 15.

43 M. V. Fox, *Character and Ideology in the Book of Esther* (Columbia: University of South Carolina, 1991), 26.

44 C. Moore suggests that if this formula identifies with Xerxes the generic name Ahasuerus (lit "chief of rulers") refers to. It is true that more than one Xerxes reigned in Persia. There are several inscriptions that follow the name of the known king, and with the descriptions of the extent of his reign. But the identity of the king is not in question, the extend of his sovereignty is. Herodotus (1:134) states that the Persians ascribed national honour according

palace, and guests in Vv.1-9 signifies the status of the kingdom. Social distinction is seen in the superior status that demands obedience of the vassal, client, wife, child and slave who are under authority. The hierarchy is easily weakened when king's subordinates refuses to comply with his demands. When denied, the claim of status one becomes a mere object of vanity, of ridicule, and contempt.[45]

3.3.1. *Traditional Interpretation*

Traditionally within the Christian and Jewish circle, Queen Vashti is seen as an unsuccessful heroine in an early struggle for women's dignity. There are many ways of reading the story of Vashti. Readers through history have tended to ignore Vashti and characters like her in the biblical texts.

According to Elsa Tamez the old anti- women custom of Hebrew culture is acknowledged as sacred, and because certain text hold to the biblical principles to prove the marginalisation of women as natural in daily life reinforces women's subordinate position.[46]Seldom, do they talk about Hagar, who is a 'negative model.'[47] Vashti is a negative model in this regard. Women who do not fit the model that the patriarchal society holds as acceptable roles to follow tend to be downplayed in the text. Thus when women read the Bible, they come up against the problem of the clear marginalisation in the various passages of scriptures.[48]

---

to the geographical extent of an empire's dominion. Carey A. Moore, "Esther, book of," *ABD,* Vol. II, 65.

45 J. Pitt Rivers, *Honour and Social Status in Honour and Shame: The Values of Mediterranean Society*, ed. J. G. Peristiany (Chicago: University of Chicago, 1965), 22.

46 Elsa Tamez, "Women's Rereading of the Bible," in *Feminist Theology from the Third World: A Reader*, ed. Ursula King (Maryknoll: Orbis Books, 1994), 192-193.

47 Kwok Pui Lan, "Racism and Ethnocentrism in Feminist Biblical Interpretation," in *Searching the Scriptures: A Feminist Introduction*, ed. Elisabeth Schüssler Fiorenza (New York: Crossroad Publishing, 1993), 105.

48 Maria Clara Bingemer, "Women in the Future of the Theology of Liberation," *Feminist Theology from the Third World: A Reader*, ed. Ursula King (Maryknoll: Orbis Books, 1994), 310.

Ancient Jewish commentators were especially critical of Vashti, maintaining that she, a grand daughter of wicked Nebuchadnezzar, was a woman of poor character. Some rabbis thought that she had been asked to appear with only the crown, that is nude (1:11). The constantly negative portrayal of Vashti in Rabbinic sources highlights the contrasting virtues of Queen Esther, who was a Sabbath observant. Vashti had forced Jewish girls to violate the Sabbath; and ultimately it was for this reason that she had been punished. Just as she caused the daughter of Israel to be stripped naked[49] and to work on the Sabbath, so was the command to appear naked her downfall.[50] This Talmudic passage consistently demeans Vashti. In Rabbinic tradition her motivation for refusing Ahasuerus's command had nothing to do with noble virtues such as modesty.

The *Second Targum* (224, 27; 237, 30) says the king commanded her to appear naked wearing only the crown.[51] Such walking naked entailed double shame as part of the socialization process in Israel; it involves awareness that public nakedness was inappropriate and unacceptable.[52] For the Persians, to show oneself in an assembly was very indecent. For it is seen that a married women could participate in Persian feasts, but when the drinking began, they would leave and give way to concubines.By coming to the king's party Vashti would degrade herself to the position of a concubine.[53] The rabbis of the *Midrash* were not sympathetic to the fate of the queen. This

---

49 This kind of misogynistic treatment of a foreign woman who is perceived as threatening recalls biblical and extra biblical traditions concerning Jezebel, among others. It should also be noted that these same traditions often view Ahasuerus as profaner as well (Meg 12a; Panim Aherim 58; Abba Gorion 9; cited in L. Ginzberg, *The Legends of the Jews* (Philadelphia: Jewish Publication Society, 1941), IV.

50 *Ibid.*, 1V, 386.

51 As quoted by Lewis B. Paton, *A Critical and Exegetical Commentary on the Book of Esther* (Edinburgh: T & T Clark, 1908), 22.

52 L. M. Bechtel, "Shame as a Sanction of Social Control in Biblical Israel: Judicial, Political and Social Shaming," *JSOT* 49 (1991), 76.

53 E. J. Bickerman, "The Colphon of the Greek Book of Esther," *JBL* 63 (1944), 186.

attitude can partly be explained on the grounds of their belief in divine justice. However, the rabbinic vilification of Vashti cannot be explained entirely as a manifestation of male chauvinism because the Jewish sages view the heroes and villain of the Bible not as individuals but as instances of recurrent historical patterns.[54] Vashti had also exposed the vulnerabilities and fragile dependencies of this patriarchal order.[55]

Midrash Esther Rabbah also depicts the negative portrayal of Vashti. One Midrash creates for her a vicious character, stating that the reason Memucan hated her was because she tried to strike him across the face with her shoe. A variant says that it was because she failed to invite his wife to the woman's banquet.[56] *Panim Aherim* states that she was killed not because of her actions but because she would become a role model of a rebellious wife and threaten the dominance of the husband throughout the realm.[57]

There were only few instances among the traditional interpreters that show Vashti in a more favourable light. In one case, she fights against the humiliation of being displayed naked without the text making any moral judgment against her.[58] There are two examples indicating that Vashti did not deserve death because it had been decreed by heaven that the descendants of Nebuchadnezzar would be expunged.[59]

Within the Christian tradition, Vashti has always been depicted as the one who wronged the king, and not the other way round.

---

54 www.wujs.org.il/activist/activities/programs/purim/eappendix.html (accessed January 12, 2003).

55 K. Timothy Beal, "Esther," in *Berit Olam: Studies in Hebrew Narrative and Poetry*, ed. David W. Cotter (Collegevill: Liturgical Press, 1999), 16.

56 Jacob Neusner, *The Components of the Rabbinic Documents from the Whole to the Parts. 11, Esther Rabbah* (Atlanta: USF Academy Commentary Series, 1997), 6-7.

57 As quoted by Leila Leah Bronner, "Esther Revisited: An Aggadic Approach," in *A Feminist Companion To Esther, Judith And Susanna*, ed. Athalya Brenner (Sheffield: Sheffield Academic Press, 1995), 190.

58 *Esther Rabbah*, 14.

59 *Ibid.*, 4.12.

Martin Luther advised husbands whose wives were disobedient, "If she still refuse, get rid of her, take an Esther and let Vashti go, as king Ahasuerus did."[60] Thus, Vashti is depicted as a rebellious queen in all the traditional interpretation; the label given to her has survived till today. It is only when interpretation is done through new perspectives that we can go beyond these traditional interpretations.

3.3.2. *Interpreting Vashti as a Feminist Heroine*

While Rabbinic tradition was almost consistently derogatory in its depiction of Vashti. Today her rebellion has made her a new role model for the contemporary woman.[61] Vashti is a marginalized character par excellence.

The image one derives of Vashti is dependent upon one's starting point. This can be seen from the patriarchal perspective of interpretations, which was quick to assign much blame and negativity to Vashti than to the king. And yet, in all these texts and interpretations, one can find something new.[62] Vashti's refusal for feminist means more today than ever before, given the work in the later half of the twentieth century toward the recovery of women's voices and women's ways of knowing and interpreting the world, which leads to a new way of reading the Bible.[63]

In interpreting we must see that there are structural problems that go beyond individual actions. The foundations and constructs

60 Carey A. Moore, *Women in Scripture: A Dictionary of Named and Unnamed Women in the Hebrew Bible, the Apocryphal/Deuterocanonical Books and the New Testament,* ed. Carol Meyers et al. (New York: Houghton Wifflin Company, 2000), 167.

61 M. Gendler, "The Restoration of Vashti," *The Jewish Woman,* ed. E. Koltun (New York: Schochen Books, 1976), 241-247.

62 The Bible in many ways are alien and antagonistic to modern women's identity, yet in other ways, it inspires and compels that identity' Cf. Renita J. Weems, "Reading her Ways through the struggle," in *Stony the Road we Trod: African-American Biblical Interpretation,* ed. Cane Hope Felder (Philadelphia: Fortress Press, 1991), 59.

63 A reading of the scripture that truly liberates responds to the situation that has motivated the reading. Cf. Tamez, "Women's Re-reading of the Bible,"190.

of society must also be challenged, especially patriarchy which cannot form a just society.[64] Vashti then becomes a symbol of resistance and a symbol of recapturing one's voice. The story of Vashti is rewritten in the hearing, the taking to heart, and changes wrought when those by saying no give us the power to say yes.[65] Vashti speaks for the powerless, those disenfranchised by gender, race, sexual orientation, or any other characteristic upon which the powerful build exclusions. Vashti was confronted with something she considered to be injustice, thus she refused to participate in her own oppression.

Others applaud Vashti's boldness viewing her as heroic, the first women in the Bible even though a 'pagan' to refuse to be treated as either a chattel or a sex object. She was a queen who in the ideology of male dominance sets for women a fine example of female independence, assertiveness and a high concept of self worth. Vashti's action marks her as a threat to the status quo of patriarchal power, and thus she is eliminated and banished. In tradition it was not uncommon to assume 'arrogant' wives as guilty.[66]

Gender related issues emerge strongly in the Book of Esther. Its heroine is a woman who offers a particular model for success, as one who opposes. Opposition works subtly behind the scenes, ultimately strengthening the power structure. Thus, in Vashti a number of modern feminist writers find their heroine. On the other hand the man, the king who banishes Vashti, receives no sympathy from the writer, he eats, drinks and follows the advise of others. His courtiers fear that Vashti will become a model of resistance for all wives. Others have pointed justifiably to the humorous tone here. The king's decision to find replacement for Vashti is introduced by an erotic suggestion in 2.1 as 'the king remembered what Vashti used

---

64 Ranjini Rebera, "Challenging Patriarchy," *Feminist Theology from the Third World: A Reader*, 106.

65 Gary David Comstock, *Gay Theology without Apology* (Cleveland: Pilgrim Press, 1993), 57-58.

66 A misogynistic Norwegian tale of the husband who kills his shrew wife and throws her in the river, where her body floats upstream. In Norwegian tale ' The Old woman against the stream' a tale collected by P. S. Asbjorsen & J. Moe, *Norwegian Folktales* (New York: Viking, 1960), 112-14.

to do for him'. Here what the king misses is not the person but a function. This leads to the understanding of the king's shallowness, which is portrayed as the stupid, impotent king.[67] Thus, Ahasuerus becomes a passive and manipulated tool in the Esther narrative. In Ahasuerus we see a good example of a bad and foolish ruler.[68]

This command is not important merely as a royal decree, but as a means by which Ahasuerus seeks to turn his queen into a spectacle of female sexuality. Queen Vashti is sacrificed on the altar of the King's machismo. Vashti is the first, but not the last, to transgress the boundaries respected and established by the patriarchal society of the Book of Esther.[69] The king now at the height of his glory gave the party and sent for Vashti to show the people.[70] The king's request here is another attempt to assert his secure control over every aspect of his reign-that is, his secure positions the true patriarch and absolute centre of the entire social order. In all this Vashti was treated exclusively as an object. She was to be brought by the eunuchs and stared at by the king and other men for pleasure.

Vashti defied her king, and her husband, by refusing to shame herself in public because the more women deny their sexuality the more honourable they are. But, according to patriarchal ideology, feminine shame as a positive value is characterized by deference and submission to male authority, by docile and timorous behaviour, by hiding nakedness, by modesty in attire and deportment.

---

67 Susan Niditch, "Esther: Folklore, Wisdom, Feminism and Authority," in *A Feminist Companion to Esther Judith and Susanna,* ed. Athalya Brenner (Sheffield: Sheffield Academic Press,1995), 33-34.

68 S. Talmon, "Wisdom in the Book of Esther," *VT* 13 (1963), 419-55, 450-51, 441-443.

69 www.english.upenn.edu/~lwarner/esth.html (accessed January 12, 2003).

70 As the king was at the height of glory, the people were supposed to get anything they wanted at the party. They probably believed that Ahasuerus was a generous king. If he refused, the people at the party would think that he was lying, thereby he would lose the respect of all these people who he had worked so hard to impress. He therefore sends the order to Vashti that she should appear in front of him wearing only the royal crown. Cf. www.torah.org/learning/yomtov/purim/5756/vol.1 No.68.html (accessed January 12, 2003).

Vashti's is not only banishment because of her disobedience, but more because of the potential effects of her disobedience. If Vashti was not punished, her decision could be the start of a major revolution. While some historical critics dismiss these details of the story, others suggest that the society, which produced them, could have been involved in great social turmoil. Women perhaps of wealth, leisure, and prestige were perhaps influenced by the women of surrounding cultures, and may have been in the process of challenging the traditional roles.[71]

The king's order is an attempt to secure his position as absolute center of the entire social order. Entertaining the men would not only affect the human dignity of Vashti, but also her vocational role within the hierarchic structure of the empire. To the King, Vashti was only a sex object to be displayed. For him there was no question of Vashti's position as queen, she was merely a woman who had to comply with the wishes and whims of a man who had power over her

Vashti was willing to give up her status and position as queen in order to do what was right. Her dignity was of more importance than her ties in the society. Perhaps Vashti knew in her heart that woman's right to assert herself is fundamentally more important than being the queen of the realm.[72] The king suffered from his obsession with manipulative power while Vashti exhibited the power of rightness.[73] Vashti as queen functions autonomously within the sphere of wombs, however, the extend of power and authority swiftly becomes clear. The moment she opposes her husband, the king, the entire machinery of the status descends on her head, and she loses all status and power.[74]

---

71 Alice L. Laffey, *Wives, Harlots and Concubines: The Old Testament in Feminist Perspective* (Philadelphia: Fortress Press, 1988), 214.

72 Knight, *Esther, Song of Songs, Lamentations: Introduction and Commentary*, 28.

73 *Ibid.*, 308.

74 Sidnie White Crawford, "The Book of Esther," in *The New Interpreters Bible: A Commentary in Twelve Volumes*, Vol. 111, ed., Leander Eeck et al. (Nashville: Abingdon Press, 1988), 883.

The reason that Vashti must be portrayed as evil is the embellishment of myth, legend and tradition that has no textual basis. The identity of Vashti as arrogant does not lie with the problem of the Bible but what it teaches. While suggestions are made justifiably to change the text itself in order to make it more modern and readable and less sexist, they could hardly object to altering the way it is taught so that Vashti can be seen less brave or at least not evil in her defiance of the king.[75]

Vashti has become one of the favourite heroines of the Jewish feminist movement. The maligned queen as a positive role model, dared to disregard the royal decree that would have her displayed as a sex object before king Ahasuerus's rowdy drinking companions. Her ultimate downfall should accordingly be viewed as martyrdom to the cause of sexual equality.

3.4. Exegetical Study of Esther 2:1-17

Chapter 1 concludes with the formation of a plan designed to restore the king's honour and to protect male honour throughout the empire. The plan involves the exile of Vashti and the proclamation of the edict. But her absence creates a vacuum in the king's court and in his heart as well. The king's honour cannot be fully restored until she is replaced. To meet this need, a contest [76] is organized to give the king

75 www.wujs.org.il/activist/activities/(programs/purim/esther/html (accessed January 12, 2003).

76 Ancient historians insist that Persian queens were chosen from select royal families. According to Herodotus (111. 84) Amestris was the queen at that time. She was the daughter of an influential Persian general. For exception to these practices a number of folk parallels to Esther's beauty and the king's contest has been mentioned and the attractiveness of this Jewish figure is viewed best as a common biblical motif. 'יפה' is used of women: Sarah (Gen. 12:11,14), Rachel (Gen. 29:17), Tamar (2 Sam.13:1; 14:27) and Abishag (1 Kgs.1:3,4); and of men: David (1 Sam. 16:12;25:3) and Absalom (2 Sam. 13:1;14:27) and Absalom (2 Sam.14:25). The specific coupling of 'תאר' with 'יפה' is found with reference to Joseph (Gen. 39:6), Abigail (1 Sam. 25:3) and the community of Israel (Jer. 11:6). The other phrase for beauty used for Esther in 2:7 which is also used for Vashti in 1:11. The description of Esther's beauty in LXX (5:1ff)

his choice among all the virgins of the land. So that he will find one "better than Vashti" (1:19).[77]

This process of appointing a new queen adds the impression that absolute power is expressed mainly as the power of men over women. Many lovely virgins from all over the whole empire were brought to the harem, where they undergo a yearlong treatment of bodily beautification to suit the king's desires. Esther is among them and when she won the contest and became the queen, it was already the seventh year of Ahasuerus reign. William Phipps points to this striking element of time: "Evidently Ahasuerus enjoys judging the contest, for four years elapse from the time that Vashti is deposed until someone is selected to take her place. He perhaps deflowered hundreds of virgins before deciding which damsel had given him the most pleasure."[78]

In the Persian empire of King Ahasuerus men had absolute power over the women and against this sexist backdrop, an ethnic drama unfolds.

3.4.1. *Esther in the King's Harem* (Vv. 1-14)

V. 2: The King's " personal attendants" had a proposal: search for the most beautiful virgins in the kingdom and let the king choose a new queen. Though this stands like a beauty contest, it was not a very happy assignment for most of the women. They were uprooted from

are more expansive. This should also be compared with the attractiveness of Susanna and Judith in Sus.2 and Judith 8:7. Cf. Herodotus, *Histories.* 111. 84

77 Lanaik, *Shame And Honour in the Book of Esther,* 59.

78 W. E. Phipps, *Assertive Biblical Women* (Westport & London: Greenwood Press, 1992), 96.

their communities, which implied confinement to the king's harem[79], and moved to what would actually be perpetual widowhood.[80]

V. 3: "Beauty treatment" included purification and the use of precious ointments[81] like the garden and the banquet hall; Ahasuerus had great appreciation for beautiful things. Unfortunately "the things" are exactly what Ahasuerus thought women were. As Vashti had shown and Esther would show, the women were as courageous and intelligent as the men in this story. In fact, both Esther and Vashti showed that they had much more respect for the dignity of life than did the king and Haman.

V. 3: Commentators speculate about how many girls were brought. Josephus claims that there were four hundred. Paton

---

79 At the beginning of the Neo-Assyrian and Neo-Babylonian periods, king of the eastern empire employed eunuchs for certain tasks, like the supervision of the royal harem or the royal children. Since these tasks were previously assigned to "normal" palace attendants, the title *saresi* acquired the technical meaning eunuch, as several cuneiform inscriptions show. Thus, the meaning eunuch arose with the practice of utilizing castrated men in key position in Assyria, Babylon and Persia. Cf. *Theological Word Book of the Old Testament,* 2 Vols, eds. R. L. Harries, Gleason L. Archer, and Bruce Waltke (Chicago: Moody Press, 1980), 635. The eunuchs played the most important role in the Assyrian bureaucracy and were numerous.They were highly trained in the Neo-Assyrian periods and in the royal palace. Cf. *New International Dictionary of Old Testament Theology and Exegesis,* Vol. 3, ed. Willem A. Van Gimeren (Nashville: Paternoster Press, 1997), 289.

A major institution in the Assyrian court was the harem, which consisted of number of wives, concubines, serving maids, and harem guards. There was a strict order of prudence within the harem, with then queen mother at the top and the chief wife of the reigning king under her. Princes normally spent their early years in the harem. There was much rivalry and jealousy within the Assyrian harem, and since the heir to the throne spent his early years then harem plots to overthrow the king was not uncommon. Cf. A. K. Grayson, "Mesopotamia, History of," *ABD*, Vol. 4, 747-750.

80 Breneman, "Esther," 314.

81 C. F. Keil, *Esther* (Grand Rapids, MI: William B. Eerdmans Publishing Company, 1980), 333.

calculates that if the king had a different girl each night for four years, there would have been 1,460.[82]

In the sentence, "Esther was also taken," we are not told whether the girls were given a choice, but we may assume that they were not. One Targum says that she was taken forcibly. As noted above for most of the girls it was not a very happy experience. When Hegai took Esther under his custody the phrase "good in his eyes and she elicited his kindness" (2:9). Kindness, חסד is usually 'done/shown' (עשׂה) to someone and, thus, something received. Favour is usually found (מָצָא) an idiomatic expression which emphasizes passivity and respect. Three times in Esther 2, the queen –to-be actively acquires the benevolence of her male superiors.[83]

V. 8: At the King's command many girls are brought to the harem in Susa. Esther is one of them. However, the author mentions that Esther is not brought to Susa but to the king's house. Does the author want to suggest a difference between Esther and other girls? Does the author already know the result of the beauty contest? Esther and the other girls are put in Hegai's[84] custody. Hegai is presented as the guardian of women. In half a verse, the 'girls' have become 'women'. It appears that 'putting girls in Hegai's hands' means the same as 'becoming a woman'. Thus Hegai evidently has something to do with the transition from girlhood to womanhood.[85] In this

82 Lewis Bayles Paton, *The Book of Esther* (Edinburgh: T & T Clark, 1908), 172-173.

83 Esther literally "takes" (נשׂא) or better, "elicits" or "wins" kindness (חסד) and favor (חֵן). In 2:9 she wins חסד from Hegai, in 2:15 she wins חֵן from "all who saw her" and in 2:17 she wins חן and חסד from the king. Cf. Lanaik, *Shame and Honour in the Book of Esther*, 63-64.

84 The eunuch Hegai was in charge of the harem of the young virgins (2:3). While eunuchs are usually associated with the king's harems and queen's attendants, they also played important roles in administrative affairs. Thus, Ahasuerus employed seven eunuchs as attendants to carry out menial tasks and errands (1:10,12,15; 6:14; 7:9).

85 Kristin De Troyer, "An Oriental Beauty Parlour: An Analysis of Esther 2.8-18 in the Hebrew, the Septuagint and the Second Greek Text," in *A Feminist Companion To Esther, Judith And Susanna*, ed. Athalya Brenner (Sheffield: Sheffield Academic Press, 1995), 49-50.

verse the women are not represented as active individuals but they are transported. Not one woman opposes this passive pattern or the text does not reflect any sign of protest. We can wonder why the girls did not go spontaneously to the palace. Perhaps this did not fit in with the culture.

V. 9: Esther appears to please Hegai, who is the central figure. He represents the 'demands' of the society and the king. In this verse Esther passes a first 'test', she enters the palace and obtains the favour of Hegai, the guardian of the women. What does she do to obtain this favour? Nothing. We read 'and the maiden pleased Hegai' and thus won his favour. Because Esther pleases Hegai he immediately gives her all the necessary adornment and food. This gives the impression that a woman thrives on food and adornment. Hegai gives her the seven best slaves and the best quarters in the harem. Esther is now in the king's house, with the best rooms and the slaves. Thus Esther is already the king's property. [86] To the author it is evident that the woman shares the opinion of the men.

V. 10: Another normative person is Mordecai. He has forbidden Esther to speak of her origins, and she obeys. Esther listens to Mordecai. By her very movements that is, 'telling nothing,' she obeys the order and norm of a man. This verse contrasts the difference between Esther's not telling and Mordecai's orders.[87] Mordecai pronounces a command to her and she obeys. The woman's identity as it is related to her ethnicity, is not very important at this point of the story. A woman can even become a queen while the king does not know where she originally comes from. On the other hand, one could also argue that Esther's identity in general is developmentally on such a low level that it becomes easy to have her hide even her ethnic background.[88] In the words of Sasson "she is pretty and winsome:

86 Kristin De Troyer, "An Oriental Beauty Parlour: An Analysis of Esther 2.8-18 in the Hebrew, the Septuagint and the Second Greek Text," in *A Feminist Companion To Esther, Judith And Susanna*, ed. Athalya Brenner (Sheffield: Sheffield Academic Press, 1995), 50.

87 *Ibid.*, 50.

88 Wyler, "The Incomplete Emancipation of a Queen," 114.

but she responds to what others expect of her. She becomes a queen because she lets others make decision crucial to her future, and she can be browbeaten by Mordecai's threat even when assured of her husband's attachment."[89]

V. 11: Esther now has beautiful quarters, good slaves, food and all types of adornment. Mordecai knows what is to be done with women. He never fails to ask two things, first how she is being prepared for the night with the king and later business is determined by food, adornment, slaves and good quarters.[90]

Vv. 12-14: indicates the process used to present the girls to the king. Apparently most of the girls spent only one night with the king. They moved on to the house of Shaashgaz,[91] where they were concubines. There was no guarantee that the king would call them again, so many were confined to virtual widowhood. Again we see how the king could use so many human beings just to satisfy his personal desire. Ahasuerus' abuse of power is evident in the demise of so many innocent women for his physical pleasure.[92]

V. 12: Literally, the first part of v.12 reads as follows: 'Now when the turn came for each maiden to go in to the King Ahasuerus at the end of the time of/the being for her, as/according to the law of women, the twelve months…'Normally after the expression 'at the end of" follows a reference to time. Here, the indication of time is split up. First we find an infinitive construct of היה and is translated as at the end (מקצ) of the time reserved for her and further indicates the real indication of time of twelve months. In between we find 'according to the law of women' which presents the ritual is something prescribed by women. The ritual is 'according to the law of women'. Two readings are possible in addition to 'the law of women', we read

89 J. M. Sasson, "Esther," *The Literary Guide To The Bible*, eds., R. Alter & F. Kermode (Cambridge: Harvard University Press, 1987), 227.

90 Troyer, "An Oriental Beauty Parlour: Anaysis of Esther 2.8-18 in the Hebrew, the Septuagint and the Second Greek Text," 51.

91 Shaashgaz was in charge of the harem of the concubines (2:14-15).

92 David J. A. Clines, *The Esther Scroll: The Story of the Story* (Sheffield: Universityy of Scheffield, 1984), 318.

as 'the law for women'. In Esther we find expressions such as 'the laws of Medes and Persians', the law of the king, the law of the Lord and the like.

The Book of Esther speaks either of law in the abstract (1.8,13,15; 3.14,15; 4.8,11,16; 8.13, 14; 9.14) or a pacific law: the law of the Persians and Medes (1.19), the word of the kings and the laws 94.3; 8.17; 9.1; 2.8), the law of the king (3.8), the law of today (9.13) their (the Jews) laws (3.18).[93] The reference to the 'laws' of women in Esther 2.12 is surprising. Whether this refers to a tradition of laws made by women or whether this should be interpreted as a slip or whether the author merely means that what is happening to the girls is totally in accordance with the law of the land. It is more a law for women than of women.[94] Because this text speaks about a rule, familiar to the eunuchs and probably Mordecai. It appears more a law for or about women, prescribed by men, and not a law prescribed by women for themselves.

V. 14: Verse 14 relates Esther's test. In the evening she will go to the King and in the morning she will return. When she returns she will go to another harem where she will be under the care of Shaashgaz, the king's eunuch who is in charge of the king's concubines. In other words, after one night with the king, Esther no longer belongs with the maidens, but with the concubines. She will not return to the king unless he is pleased with her and summons her by name. That is the lot of women in the harem.[95]

The beauty treatment, together with the night with the king, is the second last test which Esther must pass. In order to be crowned as a queen the beauty treatment is essential, it is the primary means of passing the test. Mordecai knows the procedure so also the men. The women who undergo the beauty treatment may sleep with the king,

93 In all these cases we are referring with the laws of the kings, peoples or institutions. In the ancient East legislative power lies in the hands of men. In general women were not presupposed to participate in legislative work.

94 Troyer, "An Oriental Beauty Parlour: Anaysis of Esther 2.8-18 in the Hebrew, the Septuagint and the Second Greek Text," 52-53.

95 *Ibid.*, 53.

and are put under the charge of another guardian, and may return to the king when summoned. All the active roles clearly belong to the men. They determine the course of the story. They invent the norm for the girl's lives.[96]

3.4.2. *Esther Becoming Queen* (Vv. 15-17)

Vv. 15-16: The author relates what she does in vv. 15-16. She brings with her to the king only what the eunuch advises. Hegai knows what the king likes being a man himself, he knows the norm. Esther conforms to this norm by taking only what Hegai recommended. Apparently his choice is not so bad, for she finds favour in the eyes of the king and all those who see her. Hegai expresses what all the men considers acceptable and thus he functions as the norm holder for the ritual. Esther is seen as active here as she goes to the king but her active role is identified in linked with fact that she is someone's daughter. Thus, she is defined by her relationship to the men in her life and by remaining in Mordecai's shadows.[97] Esther became the object of public male gaze. She is the viewed object, not the subject, of her story. She is not asked for her opinion and does not give it.

V. 17: The king loved Esther more than all the other women and found favour and compassion in his sight more than all the virgins. He set the royal crown on her head. The Greek text also changes an element of the repetitive parallel of Hebrew description 'and she has found 'favour' and 'compassion' in his eyes.' The Septuagint replaces this with a new parallelism. Esther finds favour in the king's eyes as she found favour in those of the eunuch. Here, the royal power is not to be compared with the power of women. The royal crown belongs to the king. Here, the author avoids giving women anything to do with the symbols of government or royal power.

---

96 Troyer, "An Oriental Beauty Parlour: Anaysis of Esther 2.8-18 in the Hebrew, the Septuagint and the Second Greek Text," 53.

97 *Ibid.*, 54.

3.5. Interpretation of the Identity of Esther

The girls whom they collected from all over the provinces were young virgins נערה בולה (2:14) probably in their early teenage, not even of marriageable age. If this is the case then the writer must have used עלמה. After collecting these young virgins, they are put in the harem for a year. All these girls may not have come for the contest of their own free will, and this is obvious because in the Jewish culture a woman does not have any say. This is also obvious in the case of Esther who was brought to the harem by her uncle Mordecai.

One by one they were called to the king in the evening and sent back in the morning. The king must have tested the girls by sleeping with them and sent them back to the harem to be his concubine. This portrays the sexual exploitation of the weaker section by the male dominated society. If the king is pleased with the girl, then she will be called again (2:14). One wonders, what would be the position of the girl, whether she could go back to her family once she was branded as the King's concubine. The plight and helpless position of those girls who could not make their fortune was serious. Though they were benefited by the royal food, the royal cosmetics and wardrobe, all these are external things in life. Internally they lost their dignity and identity. Thus, though the storywriter portrays Esther as a heroine on the one hand her position and her identity is totally oppressed and dehumanised on the other hand. Thus according to Carey Moore "Esther was called queen, but she did not rule, even after being queen for five years (3.7). Esther still occupied a weak and precarious position, in her own eyes at least, for she was most uncertain about her fate and her powers over the king."[98]

This episode is offensive to many modern commentators female or male, Jewish or Christian, because women were apparently used strictly for the pleasure of the king. Thus, the text gives no thought to the question of women's desires or wishes. However, in defence of

98 C. A. Moore, "Esther," *ABD,* Vol. II, 18.

the Book of Esther, the author uses the reality of the powerlessness of women in the Persian society. [99]

3.5.1. *Traditional Interpretation*

In the traditional interpretation, Esther's character is always depicted in contrast to the character of Vashti. Esther's character of submission and obedience are highlighted as qualities that women should possess as against those of Vashti. The traits, characters and the actions that make her successful are those that a Jew must emulate if he or she is to be successful in the world of the Diaspora. The Jews in Diaspora were clearly in a subordinate position under the Persian Empire. The Jews had to adjust since they had no political and economic power. Esther is seen as the deliverer of her people and a role model for this adjustment.[100]

3.5.2. *Esther as a Feminist Heroine*

Although, the Book of Esther takes its name from its chief female protagonist, the character of Esther has suffered much in the history of interpretation. Scholars insist that Mordecai is the primary hero of the book, because of the fact that at the time of crisis, it was Mordecai, who went to Esther to ask her to intercede with the king. Thus, Esther devises a plan and carries it out with admirable skill. Without Esther there would have been no story but Feminist scholars always prefer the deposed Vashti over Esther. Esther is considered

---

99 They were taken from their homes, put in the harem, given a year of special beauty treatments and taken to spend the night with the king. If they managed to titillate his sexual appetite, they may be called back, if not they were locked away in the second harem, never to be seen again for they were the property of the king. They could not approach the king unless the king asked. Cf. Sidnie White Crawford, "Esther," in *Women in Scripture: A Dictionary of Named and Unnamed Women in the Hebrew Bible. The Apocryphal/Deuterocanonical Books and The New Testament* (Boston: Houghton Mifflin, 2000), 368.

100 Frank S. Frick, *A Journey through the Hebrew Scripture* (Fort Worth, Philadelphia, San Diego, New York, Orlando, Austin, San Antonio, Toronto, Montreal, London, Sydney, Tokyo: Harcourt Brace College Publishers, 1995), 475-476.

neither "woman" enough, nor "man" enough to satisfy any of her critics. But, neither of these positions does justice to the character of Esther.[101]

Esther serves a model of a successful Jew living in Diaspora. She is able to function as a model precisely because she is a woman. Within the culture, called either as 'Western' or 'Judeo-Christian,' is a culture that is admittedly male-dominated and patriarchal. Women have been the constantly marginalized and oppressed gender. Lacking public power, women have historically been able to gain individual or private strength only by successfully exploiting the male power structure around them, as Esther does so well in this story. Her actions are presented as a model for the male Jews, living in exile, or for the marginalized and powerless minority members of Persian society.[102]

In the book, at first, Esther appears either dumb or helpless. Mordecai is depicted as the one who makes her decisions. He commands her not to report that she is Jewish (2:10), he checks on her everyday, walking in front of the harem to learn of her health (2:11). Esther continues to be only a pawn in Mordecai's hand when he discovers the plot against the king. He is the active party, and Esther merely conveys a message "in the name of Mordecai" (2:22). Esther enters the story as an archetypal dependent, a female symbol of disenfranchisement, dependence, and an outsider in need of protection, resembling Ruth. In Israelite society, widows and strangers were often objects of injustice because of their liminal status outside the normal structure. They were helpless and easily oppressed, requiring legal and personal protection for their very survival,[103] which describes the gauntlet run by women before being admitted to the king. The norm for admission is physical beauty.

101 Sidnie White Crawford, "Esther: A Feminine Model for Jewish Diaspora," *Gender and Difference in Ancient Israel*, ed. Peggy L. Day (Philadelphia: Fortress Press, 1989), 161-177.

102 Sidnie White Crawford, "The Book of Esther," *The New Interpreters Bible*, Vol. III, 872-73.

103 Lanaik, *Shame and Honour in the Book of Esther,* 61.

Thus, it is assumed that the text is written by a man who states that women must please men.

The book hides women's identity, and restricts women's role transmitting a norm of behaviour, derived completely from a male point of view. Therefore, this book in all its likelihood is written by a man or at the very least from a male perspective. The Book of Esther does not provide a precise physical description of its heroine, in keeping with Israelite narrative tradition. She must be the most beautiful girl in the court because she is the king's choice. As indicated she is not chosen because of her lineage or wealth, but because of her beauty. Esther is the object of the king's gaze.

Androcentrism characterizes many commentators on Esther, and most commentators have focused on the character of Mordecai as the paradigm for Jewish life in Diaspora. Carey Moore says "between Mordecai and Esther, the greater hero is Mordecai, who supplied the brains while Esther simply followed his directions."[104] According to Paton,

> Esther for the chance of winning wealth and power takes her place in the herd of maidens who became concubines of the king. She wins her victories not by skill or by character, but by her beauty. She conceals her origin, is relentless toward a fallen enemy, and secures not merely that the Jews escape from danger, but they fall upon their enemies, slay their wives and children and plunder their property.[105]

Feminist interpreters see that obscured in Esther's character is also full compliance with patriarchy. In contrast to Vashti who refused to be men's sexual object, and her husband's toy, Esther is the stereotypical woman in a man's world. She wins favour by the physical beauty of her appearance, and then by her ability to satisfy sexually. She concentrates on pleasing those in power, that is Hegai and Ahasuerus. Her access to power is through these men only. When feminists compare the two women, they extol Vashti, though

104 Moore,"Esther,"*ABD*, Vol. II, 11.

105 Paton, "The Book of Esther,"*ICC*, 96.

they are not at all surprised that the literature, produced as it was in a patriarchal culture, honours Esther and relegates Vashti to oblivion. Feminist concern however is to reclaim Vashti.[106] But looking at the story of Esther also helps us to reclaim her as a feminist heroine who as a foreign woman had no way but to use her wisdom to challenge the patriarchal structure. The story honours Esther as a woman and as a queen, but in the author's world her honour is necessarily of a different sort than men. Hers is a muted honour[107] that maintains male dominance.[108] According to Herzfeld, Esther is honoured by the narrative for her "subversive submission to the social structure."[109]

The question whether the book deals with Esther the Jewish heroine or Mordecai the Jewish hero depends on particular reading. Interestingly in the book, it is the nationality of Mordecai that is much more explicit than that of Esther (3:3; 5:13; 8:7; 9:29, 31). One would conclude that although the book bears the name of a woman, it is actually a story about the man Mordecai (9:4) and the Jew Mordecai (3:3; 5:13). It is thus a national male story. Mosal is right when he argues that, in the Book of Esther, Esther is used to achieve the national male agenda.[110] Thus White argues that,

> The Jews in the Diaspora are in the position of the weak, as a subordinate population under the dominant Persian Government. They must adjust to their lack of immediate political and economic power and learn to work within the system to gain what power they can. Esther made

106 Laffey, *Wives, Harlots and Concubines: The Old Testament in Feminist Perspective,* 216.

107 E. Ardener, "Belief and the Problem of Women," *Perceiving Women*, ed. S. Ardener (London: Malaby, 1975), 1-17.

108 P. Sanday, *Female Power and Male Dominance: On the Origins of Sexual Inequality* (New York: Cambridge University, 1981), 61.

109 Lanaik, *Shame and Honour in the Book of Esther,* 165.

110 Mmadipoane Masenya (Ngwana 'Mphahlele) "Esther and Northen Sotho Stories and an African-South African Women's Commentary," in *Other Ways of African Woman and the Bible,* ed. Musa W. Dube (Geneva: WCC Publications, 2001), 30.

> the adjustment. Not only is she a woman, a member of a perpetually subordinate population, but also she is an orphan, a powerless member of Jewish society. Therefore, her position is constantly precarious, as was the position of the Jews in Diaspora. With no native power of her own owing to her sex or position in society, Esther must learn to make her way among the powerful and to cooperate with others in order to make herself secure.[111]

This passage is disturbing to the modern reader and particularly troubling to women. Hundreds of young girls are rounded up, their wishes not consulted or even considered. Placed in a strange locale away from their family and friends; subjected willingly or unwillingly, to a series of "treatments" and then given one night for the pleasure of one man. What makes it even worse is that the text contrary to expectations does not adopt a condemnatory attitude, but rather accepts the process as part of the status quo. In fact, the heroine is applauded from her success in the process and her eventual triumph in the contest. It is difficult to take the position of Paton, who remarked above that Esther took her chance by using her beauty in the herd of the maidens for wining wealth and power.[112]

However, such a dismissal of Esther's character would be doing the book damage. The text of the Hebrew Bible is besieged with stories of doubtful morality and we do not discard them. Esther's action must be judged within the social and cultural parameters of her story and within those parameters[113] that confine her to her identity as mere object.

111 Sidnie White Crawford, "Esther," *The Women's Bible Commentary*, ed. Carol A. Newsom and Sharon H. Ringe (Louisville: Westminster John Knox Press, 1992), 167.

112 Paton, "The Book of Esther,"*ICC* , 96.

113 Crawford, "The Book of Esther," 890.

Summary

Thus women's identity is seen as imposed upon from ancient times. These stereotypical identities have been passed on, until we have them in our midst today. A patriarchal society is based on the belief that male is the superior sex and many of the social institutions and social practices is organized to reflect this belief; in one sense a patriarchal society is organized so that the belief in male supremacy 'comes true.'[114] Ahasuerus is seen here as an ultimate patriarchal authority in relation to female. Thus, the book clearly pictures the patriarchal society that has shaped the identities of these two women. This restriction existed only because of their gender. Probably the only activity they were assigned and though capable for was the tending of their homes, and looking after their families, which actually is one of the hardest task in the society. To consider that a woman could think for herself was a far fetch idea. Esther and Vashti's identity as female has been subjected to a place of oppression and domination, thereby interpreting them from a male perspective for the male reader.

In contrast a feminist reader views these two identities by portraying them as dominated by male ideology and draws them out from that structure to a liberative paradigm for women. In studying the Book of Esther, the aim is not to forget the courageous and shrewd acts of the women involved, for which they are remembered. However, the intention here is primarily to find out how patriarchal power dominated the identities of Esther and Vashti by viewing them as mere objects, where their characters have been confined to the tags of 'body' as beautiful and fair. In this book, both women are to be seen as not in opposition to each other's identity, but as supplementing each other, depending upon their context and needs.

114 Dale Spender, *Man Made Language* (London: Routledge & Kegan Paul, 1985), 3.

Chapter 4

Socio-Cultural Constructions of Women's Body
Its Implications for Re-Reading the Identity of Vashti and Esther in Today's Context

The patriarchal structure retains power in the hands of a few, by using them to violate the rights, dignity and identity of women. In such situations women are under their control and in these settings, the dependency is apparent in which women are perceived as helpless and totally disempowered.[1] This chapter seeks to identify how culture and society inscribe the body of women as mere object to be viewed and stamped upon. It also aims to compare the identity of Vashti and Esther with today's ideological concept about women labelled as an object, re-reading these women with new eyes.

1 Mary John Mananzan, "Feminist Socialization: Woman as Victims and Collaborators," *Concilium* 1(1994), 6-7.

4.1. The Understanding of Identity

Identity is concerned with the self-esteem and self-image of a community or an individual. It deals with one's personhood, position in society, and relation to others. It is the fundamental about issues of belonging, expression, performance, identification and communication with others.[2] One's identity is important not only in understanding oneself but also of its relation to others in the community.

According to Mary McGee, "Women are not just female human beings. That is, women's identities are not reducible to their biological function or even their self-awareness as sexual beings. Gender identities are entwined with and even influenced by other social identities."[3] Humans are not limited to the biological and anatomical identities of male and female, but rather burdened with various social, psychological, emotional, religious and cultural attributes, the values of which shift according to the context.[4] Circumstances often draw the loyalties of one dimension of one's identity to the foreground. Each of these multiple identities of an individual is part of a structure that is often oppressive. At each moment, the individual stands in a particular location. This can be either powerful or powerless depending upon one's location at a particular time where identity gives an individual power and positions in society.

4.2. The Concept of Women's Identity

The concept of female identity is particularly important within the work of those feminists, influenced by psychoanalysis. They recognize that the identity of female is the result of patriarchal structure and this results in viewing women as an object to be used and controlled by patriarchal power. Sigmund Freud has argued that the child gains a sense of identity within a social order through identification with the

2 K. Hetherington, *Expressions of Identity: Space, Performance Politics* (New Delhi: Sage Publications, 1998), 62.

3 M. Leslie & Mary McGee eds., *Invented Identities: The Interplay of Gender, Religion and Politics in India* (New Delhi: Oxford University Press, 2000), 33.

4 Hetherington, *Expressions of Identity: Space, Performance, Politics,* 34.

father, a process which leaves girls estranged from their mothers and identifying with a power which is not their own.[5] French feminists such as Julia Kristava seek to develop a concept of feminine identity by allying it with the anarchic drives that are suppressed within the regulatory dominant order.[6]

Foucault in his book *History of Sexuality* puts forward the view that sexual behaviour, far from being innate is in fact governed by complex ideological systems. He also examines the operation of discursive power-formations, the female body, which he argues was subjected to a process of hysterisation. Identified wholly with its reproductive functions, the female subject was thus confined to the private domestic sphere.[7] Although Foucault's work was never explicitly feminist in orientation, many theorists argue that he has given feminism new ways of thinking about how women are controlled within a patriarchal system.[8]

Ethical reflection starts from the 'lived' world of experience-a pre-given world of valued relation.[9] Erikson maintained that in the social environment of human existence, psychosocial identity becomes very important in individual development.[10] Erikson also points out that sometimes social influence may not always be beneficial, since

---

5 Michael Jacobs, *Sigmund Freud* (New Delhi: Sage Publications, 1992), 53-56.

6 As quoted by Sarah Gamble, "Identity," *The Routledge Companion to Feminism and Post Feminism*, ed. Sarah Gamble (London & New York: Routledge, 2001), 252.

7 Michel Foucault, *History of Sexuality: An Introduction,* Vol. 1 (New York: Vintage Books, 1990), 84.

8 Gita Sen, "Subordination and Sexual Control: A Comparative View of the Control of Women," in *The Women Gender and Development Reader,* ed. Malini Visvanathan et al (London & New Jersey: 2nd Books Ltd, Dhaka: University Press Ltd., Bangkok: White Lotus Co. Ltd., Cape Town: David Philip, 1997), 234.

9 Gibson Winter, *Elements for Social Ethics: The Role of Social Science in Public Policy* (New York: The Macmillan Company, London: Collier-Macmillan Ltd., 1966), 218.

10 Erik H. Erikson, *A Way of Looking at Things*, ed. Stephen Schlein (New York: Norton & Company, 1987), 676.

elements of culture often confront an individual with contradictory values, so that forming a consistent sense of identity can be difficult. Societies create oppressed minorities, whose members may find themselves compelled to adopt negative identity imposed by the majority.[11] Thus, he also sees the stereotyping of women's identity as a part of the social environment.

4.3. Socio-Cultural Norms as Instruments in Formulation of Identity

Community creates human in its own image. This world of values, norms, patterns of behaviour, social roles and corresponding sanctions existed before one's birth and it changes with gradual modification during the span of one's lives. It is a pre-given world of ethical, aesthetic, technical and social understanding.[12] Humans as they relate in community live by those norms that they are taught as right and acceptable. Thus the social constructionist position on the woman's body emphasizes the view that woman experiences her body, sexuality and feminine identity as a social being located in a particular cultural setting with its dominant values and norms.[13]

4.3.1. *Imposition of Patriarchal Values: Culture and Norms*

Society distinguishes between legitimate and illegitimate conduct. Humans are not only affected by inherited traits, and external environment, but also by the cultural pattern it acquires, and the normative order, norms or control it lives under. It is through them,

---

11 Cited by Robert B. Ewen, *An Introduction to Theories of Personality*, Third Edition (New Jersey: Lawrence Erlbaum Associates Publishers, 1988), 240-241.

12 Winter, *Elements for Social Ethics: The Role of Social Science in Public Policy*, 217.

13 Menakshi Thapan, "Gender and Embodiment in Everyday Life," in *Embodiment: Essays on Gender and Identity*, ed. M. Thapan (New Delhi: Oxford University Press, 1997), 5.

that human society regulates the behaviour of its members in such a way that they perform activities fulfilling societal needs.[14]

From childhood through the process of socialization, people are confronted by gender norms, which become part of their self-identity, and whereby gender social definitions are internalized.[15]

The norms lay down the formal rights and obligations in connection with a position, permitting certain amount of legitimate variation within the limits imposed; it also lays down rules to be followed in case the individual oversteps the limits.[16]

In the modern world, cultures like media and religion are powerful institutions, which inculcate patriarchal cultural values and norms. They project women's identity in terms of a body. In the contemporary culture, through magazines, novels, internet, movies, advertisements, Music Television videos, pornography, to art galleries, women's bodies are made into popular commodities.[17] Thus, according to Margaret Atwood, "The female body has many uses. It's been used as a doorknocker, a bottle opener, as a clock within a ticking belly, as something to hold up lamp, liquor; it sells diet plans and diamonds and desire in tiny crystal bottles."[18] The commodification of women's bodies is not a recent development. The western visual tradition of the nude has been developed by a male artistic gaze and was created for male spectators. Women, as the object of men's gaze are portrayed as weak, passive, and available for

---

14 Kingsley Davies, *Human Society* (Delhi: Surjeet Publications, 1981), 52.

15 Janet Saltzman Chafetz "Gender Equality: Towarda Theory of Change," in *Feminism and Sociological Theory: Key Issues in Sociological Theory*, ed. Ruth A. Wallace (Newbury Park, London, New Delhi: Sage Publications 1989), 139.

16 Davies, *Human Society*, 87.

17 Margaret Atwood, "The Female Body," in *The Female Body: Figures, Styles, Speculations*, ed. Laurence Goldstein (Ann Arbor: University of Michigan Press, 1991), 2-3.

18 Joanna Fruech, "Has the Body Lost its Mind?," in *Erotic Faculties* (Berkley & Los Angeles: University of California Press, 1996), 118.

men's sexual needs.[19] The prominent cultural signs and media images dominate the way one defines oneself and the world around us.[20]

Patriarchal values are inculcated to a woman, as well as, to a man through myths, stories and proverbs. Patriarchy socializes men and women to accept their dominant and submissive positions respectively as normative in church and society.

4.3.2. *Patriarchal Ideology in Disguise as Natural Law*

The ideology of culture and social norms has been a site of struggle for feminists because it is through culture that meanings are formed and transmitted. It is in the private sphere that women establish their identity, following those things deemed appropriate for their age and gender. Women's position in society and their unique self-understanding are regarded as historically conditioned and socially constructed.[21] In any society there is the expectation of the participants, which relies to a great extend, on the norms applicable in the situation. One's behaviour is fitted according to the anticipations of the other.[22] Patriarchal conception of what is the valuable, the good and true, to a substantial degree becomes the socially accepted definitions. Social definitions are therefore, androcentric and reflect a masculine perspective of the world.[23]

19 Wioleta Polinska, "Dangerous Bodies: Women's Nakedness and Theology," *Journal of Feminist Studies in Religion* 16, no. 1 (Spring 2000), 46.

20 Natalie Fenton, "Feminism and Popular Culture," in *The Routledge Companion to Feminism and Post Feminism*, ed. Sarah Gamble (London & New York: Routledge, 2001), 109.

21 Ealine Graham, *Making the Difference, Gender, Personhood and Theology* (New York: Mowbray 1995), 53.

22 Davies, *Human Society*, 83.

23 Winter, *Elements for Social Ethics: The Role of Social Science in Public Policy*, 138.

4.3.3. *Eulogizing of Patriarchal Values*

Identity is related to environment, society, worldview and culture, and consequently related to the future and anticipated adult roles.[24] An acceptable ideology has compelling power of reliability, giving meaning and structure to life, thus having ethical and religious overtones.[25] Compliments indicate what is valued as good and ideal in society. A compliment in society often implies, that a woman has adequately fulfilled the roles expected of her in a patriarchal society. A woman is praised as the home-maker, without having any power over her own body or her sexuality or made to act as a deciding body. Therefore, women are socialised to adapt those values that the culture passes down to them.

Patriarchal culture and norms, shape the feminine body by producing the 'feminine' body as the ideal body. Women's faces and bodies are made over according to the normative standards of beauty, hence, compliance to the prevalent standards of 'feminine' dress and make-up becomes pre-requisite for well-paying jobs and social mobility.[26]

4.4. Women as Body

Religion has been one of the patriarchal structures that have objectified women and denigrated their bodies. The Bible denounce women as the 'weaker vessel,' 'created for the sake of men,' as 'inferior and unclean being.' In the second and third century, women's leadership was equated with heresy as such that the image and identity of women had negative connotations. Many of the Church Fathers accused women for the fall of human being, and they were considered as evil and deceitful.[27] At the same time, they tended to

24 J. Eugene Wither, *Erikson Identity and Religion* (New York: The Seabury Press, 1982), 71.

25 *Ibid.*, 81.

26 Elisabeth Schüssler Fiorenza & M. Shawn Copeland, *Violence Against Women* (London: SCM Press Ltd., & Maryknoll: Orbis Books, 1994), xii.

27 For Tertullian women are the Devil's Gateway, for they crush the image and law of God. Cf. Tertullian, *On the Dress of Women*, (1,1,2), trans Elizabeth

portray woman as intellectually inferior to men on account of her body.[28] It was this body that drew her away from eternal concerns leading her into temporal cares.[29] This bodily weakness was assumed to make women easy victim of deception which explains the tragic fall of the first woman.[30] Eve was called 'the author of sin' because she 'dragged her husband into sin' and became the 'devils gateway' to all humanity.[31] Eve's carnal wickedness sealed the fate of all women. Women were perceived as susceptible to sin, inherently flawed and in need of men's assistance against the weak powers of their bodies.[32] The Church fathers thus categorized women as sex symbols, sources of sin and gateway to hell. Martin Luther defines woman thus:

> God has created men with broad chests and shoulders, not lips so that men can understand wisdom but the place where

---

A. Clark, *Women in the Early Church, Message of the Fathers of the Church 13* (Collegeville, Minnesota: The Liturgical Press, 1983), 38.

According to John Chrysostom, a wife had just one purpose; to guard the possession men accumulated, to keep a close watch on the income, and to take charge of the household. Cf. John Chrysostom, "Discourse 2 on Genesis: The Kind of Women who ought to be taken as Wives (4)," Trans. in Elizabeth A. Clark, *Women in the Early Church*, 36.

28 Augustine, "*De Trinitate (*12.7)," *St Augustine: on the Holy Trinity, Doctrinal Treatises, Moral, Moral Treatises. A Select library of the Nicene and Post Nicene Fathers,* Vol. III, ed. Philip Schaff (Buffalo: The Christian Literature Company, 1887), 12.7.

29 Augustine and Henry Chadwick, *Confessions* (Oxford: Oxford University Press, 1998), 12.30.

30 Cyprian, "On the Dress of Virgins," *Cyprian. A Select library of the Nicene and Post Nicene Fathers*, ed. Philip Schaff (Grand Rapids, MI: William B. Eerdmans Publishing Company, 1956), 4:31.

31 Tertullian, "On the Apparel of Women," *Fathers of the Third Century: Tertullian part four, Minucuis, Conumodian, Origin, Part First and Second.* The Ante-Nicene Father, Vol. IV, eds. Alexander Roberts & James Donaldson, A. Cleveland Coxe (New York: Charles Scribner's Sons, 1913), 1:1.

32 John Chyrsostom, "Discourse 2 on Genesis: The Kind of Women who ought to be Taken as Wives," *Women and Religion: The Original Sourcebook of Women in Christian Thought*, ed. Elizabeth A. Clark and Herbert Richardson (San Francisco: Harper San Francisco, 1996), 36-37.

> the filth flows out is small. With women, it is the other way round; that's why they have lots of filth and little wisdom... women are created for no other purpose than to serve men and be their helpers. If women grow weary or ever die while bearing a child, that doesn't harm anything. Let them bear children to death, they are created for that.[33]

Miles argues that the prevalent concern over the inherent eroticism of woman's body shows that "the female body has been, in the societies of the christian west, are 'mastered' in representation, that viewer's most immediate reaction is to see female nakedness as an object of male desire."[34] All these views cannot be taken into account, because the body does own an identity. This body serves as an epistemological tool to analyze the experiences of women. As Elizabeth Grosz puts forward:

> The body can be regarded as a kind of threshold; it is placed between a psychic or lived interiority through the inscription of the body's outer surface... by which the body is marked, scarred, transformed and written upon or constructed by the various regimes of institutional discursive, and non discursive power as a particular kind of body...our body forms are considered as expressions of an interior, not inscription of a late surface...The body becomes a text, a system of signs to be deciphered, read, and read into. Social law is incarnated, 'corporealised,' correlatively bodies are 'textualised,' 'read' by others as expressive of a subject's psychic interior. A storehouse of inscriptions and messages between its internal and external boundaries, it generates or constructs the body's movement into "behaviour," which

33 As quoted by Mary Weisner, "Luther and Woman," in *Feminist Theology: A Reader*, ed. Ann Loades (Louisville: Westminster John Knox Press, 1990), 123.

34 Margaret R. Miles, *Carnal Knowing* (New York: Vintage, 1991), 144.

then have interpersonally and socially identifiable meanings and functions within the social system.[35]

Erving Goffman also points out, the body is important for identifying the link between people's identity and social identity.[36] The body has an identity shaped by ideologies of casteism, capitalism, and colonialism that define the identity. Thus, woman's body becomes the site of inscription, oppression, exploitation and violence. At the same time it is used as an instrument of resist, struggle, party and triumph.[37] According to Meenakshi Thapan, it is the social and historical settings where women are located, which affect the nature of their embodied experience and articulation of their identity in the Indian context.[38] The lives of Indian women lie at the edge of caste and class inequality, especially since the portrayal and management of gender and female sexuality is involved in the reproduction and defence of social inequality.[39]

---

35 Elizabeth Grosz, 'Bodies and Knowledge: Feminism and the Crisis of Reason,' in *Feminist Epistemologies*, ed. Linda Alcoff an Elizabeth Potter (New York, Routledge, 1993), 196-98.

36 Erving Goffman as quoted by Meenakshi Thapan, "Gender and Embodiment in Everyday Life," in *Embodiment: Essays on Gender and Identity* ed. M. Thapan (New Delhi: Oxford University Press, 1997), 2.

37 Evangeline Anderson Rajkumar, "Significance of the 'Body' in Feminist Theological Discourse," *BTF* XXXIII, no. 2 (December 2001), 88-89.

38 It is argued that Indian situational discourse has generated a different construction of woman's body and sexuality located in the specific issues of caste, communalism, the trauma of partition at the time of political independence, the socialization practices common to different cultures, the social practices of dowry related deaths, female foeticide and infanticide, rape of women belonging to particular communities, child marriage and so on. Cf. Thapan, "Gender and Embodiment in Everyday Life," 6.

39 Kumkum Sangari & Sudesh Vaid, eds., *Recasting Women: Essays in Colonial History* (New Delhi: Kali for Women, 1989), 5. The female sexuality is controlled by class and caste factors. A woman's body and sexuality are in any case under the controlling purview of men, but men of higher caste and classes appear to have special privileges, which may be coercively asserted. It is an assertion not only of patriarchal power but also of social control. Cf. Thapan, "Gender and Embodiment in Everyday Life," 6.

The body is an instrument used to construct sexual difference and inequality. The body of a woman is often reduced to an object of possession of a man, to be exhibited, decorated, envied and cherished.

4.5. Identity of Women as a Commodity

The notion of feminity in Television and commercials is that of commodification, by rigidly defined boundaries of existence whereby the substance of woman's being, expression and experience are reduced to a mere object.[40] Irigaray argued that this kind of commodification of women is inherent in a patriarchal system. She states that, in the social order, women are mere 'products' for use and exchanged among men. Consequently women's status becomes that of merchandise, products. "The use, consumption, and circulation of their bodies underwrite the organization and reproduction of the social order, in which they have never taken part as subjects."[41]A close analysis shows that women were commodified in four basic ways.

4.5.1. *Woman as an Object to be Viewed*

In any patriarchal culture the female body that has served as the object of sexual stimulation, in advertising as well as other forms of mass media. Kuhn argues that this cultural way of seeing a female body as a sex object has deep material and historical roots.[42] In a patriarchal society, most depictions of women connote "otherness," different from the male norm. Women are the objects of the gaze as opposed to the subject of the gaze.[43]

---

40 D. A. Yanni, "The Social Construction of Women as Mediated by Advertising," *Journal of Communication* 14 (1990), 71-81.

41 L. Irigaray, *This Sex is not One* (Ithaca: Cornell University Press, 1985), 84.

42 Kuhn argues that "whenever we look at painted, drawn, sculpted or photographed images of women, it is important for us to remind ourselves that images of women have traditionally been the province of the property of men." Cf. A. Kuhn, *The Power of Image: Essays on Representation and Sexuality* (London & Boston: Routledge & Kegan Paul, 1985), 10-11.

43 J. Berger, *Ways of Seeing* (London: British Broadcasting Corporation: Penguin Books, 1972), 47.

4.5.2. *Woman as a Signifier for the Product*

U. Stannard puts that "Glittering and smiling in the media, looked at by millions, envied and ogled, these ideal beauties teach women their role in society…. In other words, that woman are made to be looked at, and that females achieve success in the world by being looked at."[44] The female viewer /consumer is expected to have an alluring smile, luscious lips, luxuriant hair and fair complexion among other physical attributes. By using the model's body and looks, the commercial implicates her in perpetuating the male –defined ideals of beauty.[45]

4.5.3. *Woman as a Non-Thinking, Decorative Object*

A woman's sexuality is exploited not only to sell a variety of products, but also to provide visual pleasure to the viewers. As a decorative object, a woman is frequently depicted as brainless body and her body is exploited to sell products, even if these products did not have any relation to woman's body or need. Thus Xavier observed the gratuitous and irrelevant use of women's physical appearance:

> Whether it is to sell shaving cream or edible oil, milk biscuits or cigarettes, washing powder or condoms, business house *vie* with each other for the customers attention, often using scantily clad nubile young women in their advertisement campaigns to achieve this end… These women are gorgeous apparitions, representing the fantasies of a particular consumerist society. [46]

---

44 U. Stannard, "The Mask of Beauty," in *Woman in Sexist Society: Studies in Power and Powerlessness*, eds. V. Gornick & B. K. Moran (New York: Basic Books, Inc., 1971), 123.

45 Ashik Roy, *Selling Stereotypes: Images of Women in Indian Television* (New Delhi: New Concepts Information Systems Pvt. Ltd., 1998), 77.

46 C. Xavier, "Advertisements and Women," *Indian Express* 8 (1992), 8.

4.5.4. *Woman as a Fragmented Object*

J. Root showed the fragmented images of women's bodies as "each body part becomes eroticed and sexual to-be-looked-at and marvelled in. The whole outer surface of the body is transformed into an exquisite, passive thing,"[47] for the visual pleasure of the male. Fragmenting female bodies to turn them into objectives or fetishes is an important constituent of advertising. According to Mills, the fragmentation of women's bodies has two main effects: the body becomes "depersonalised, objectified, and reduced to its parts,"[48] and second, since the female model in the commercial is not represented as a "unified conscious living being, the scene cannot be focalised from her perspective."[49] Fragmentation traps a woman's sexuality with commodity relations part of a woman, her face, lips or hair signifies her whole, but these individual part also function as signifiers for the advertised products, in which she becomes the advertised commodities. V. Export argues that society defines feminity in terms of woman's body part, parts that are so interchangeable and generic that woman herself becomes interchangeable and in the process, becomes depersonalised, dehumanised and objectified.[50]

When women put on the appearances based on male standards, they are made a part of female objectification process. Thus, women are offered a sense of themselves only as defined by patriarchal systems of representation.

4.6. Problems of Identity of Women as Body

4.6.1. *Authority over the Action of Women's Body*

The body of a woman often has the obligation of being carriers of cultural traditions. Whenever men are charmed with a particular kind of identity, this results in women being burdened with more

47 J. Root, *Pictures of Women: Sexuality* (London & Boston: Pandora Press, 1984), 66.

48 S. Mills, *Feminist Stylistics* (New York: Routledge, 1995), 172.

49 *Ibid.*, 172.

50 V. Export, "The Real and its Double: The Body," *Discourse* 11 (1988), 3-27.

restrictive ways of life and cultural order like dress codes, like the Muslim women, who cover themselves in order not to lead men into temptation. Sandra Lee Bartky also points out that such socio-cultural practices produce the docile, subjected and made up body as the ideal body of feminity.[51]

Women are taught what are the acceptable gestures, postures, movements and behaviour they need to maintain. Thus, patriarchal society, conditions and controls the social behaviour of a woman by perpetuating discriminatory values as positive.[52]

4.6.2. *Authority on the Freedom of Women's Body*

Woman is allowed little or no space for an independent, self-perceived articulation and expression of her sexuality. Her body becomes an instrument and a symbol for the community's expression of caste, caste and communal honour. Thus woman's body is often taken over by the community, of both men and women, to establish and legitimise its image in society.[53] The identity and status of women are derived from their relation to the explicitly gendered categories of mothers, daughters and wives. Women are defined not only in relation to men but also as dependent on men and subordinate to men. Men on the other hand are not defined in relation to women nor in familial terms but in relation to a larger public world, in which they operate as workers, colleagues or citizens.[54]

---

51 Sandra Lee Bartky, "Foucault, Feminity, and the Modernization of Patriarchal Power," in *Feminism and Foucault, Reflections on Resistance,* eds. Irene Diamond and Lee Quinbee (Boston: Beacon Press, 1988), 61-68.

52 For example, the 'value' of silence and passivity is taken as a normative response at the time of violence. Patriarchy identifies two reasons to silence woman, as by invalidating in advance and by discrediting after the event. By describing a woman's speech as comic, gossip, lies, hysteria, and ignorance, patriarchy effectively deflects a great deal of its significance and force. Cf. Rajeshwari Sunder Rajan, *Real and Imagined Woman: Gender, Culture and Postcolonialism* (New York, London: Routledge, 1993), 88.

53 Thapan, "Gender and Embodiment in Everyday Life," 6.

54 Linda McDowell and Rosemary Pringle, eds., *Defining Women: Social Institutions and Gender Divisions* (Oxford: Polity Press, Blackwell Publishers, 1992), 3.

A woman's mobility is controlled through construction of social expectations and values. Masculine is defined as 'aggressive, bold, brave, daring, strong,' and feminine is defined as 'female, ladylike, womanly, delicate, soft and tender.' The values of an ideal woman subsequently boil down to chastity, absolute fidelity, love, patience, unconditional forgiveness and their existence only for the sake of their husbands.

4.6.3. *Authority on the Sexuality of Women's Body*

Body as a cultural constructed identity, documents how the practices of culture religion, and gender norms produces the 'feminine body'.[55] The sexuality of women in a patriarchal society is regarded as wild, insatiable and dangerous, that needs to be controlled. Women who refuse to come under the control of men are looked upon as potential devourers of family and community honour. Believing that women bring shame to themselves and their families if their sexual energies are not kept in control, many rules exist to control a woman's sexuality and behaviour in society. This shows that female sexuality is considered as a threat.[56]

According to Gita Sen, the growth of economic surplus and the development of the state developed a patriarchal household, where the control of children passed from women to men. Within the patriarchal household, the daughter in law is sexually controlled in the interests of reproducing the patriarchal hierarchy within the household, and guardians of their sexuality are older women, mothers and mothers-in-law whose own relative position is based on their ability to recruit the labour and sexuality of younger women to reproduce patriarchal domination. The role of men is to dominate and control the public space. This control, takes the form where women, especially young women are under rigidly defined, and strict

55 Mary Daly, *Gyn/Ecology, The Metaethics of Radical Feminism* (London: The Women's Press, 1987), 183-185.

56 Kalpana Viswanath, "Shame and Control :Sexuality and Power in Feminist Discourse in India," *Embodiment: Essays on Gender and Identity*, ed. M. Thapan (New Delhi: Oxford University Press, 1997), 313-333.

limits of movements, dress and action. Any transgression of these limits, by women brings swift and harsh retribution in the form of physical and sexual molestation.[57]

These gender specific histories can be questioned, criticized and challenged. As Grosz suggests that women's specificities, corporeality and subjectiveness, are not inherently resistant to depiction. In those cultures where the masculine is represents the feminine as the reverse itself, thereby the masculine relying on the subordination of the feminine. But, this is not biologically and logically fixed, so it can be contested and changed.[58] A liberal feminist holds the opinion that cultural interpretation of sex distinction results in experience, thought and practice by women with certain cultural values designated as 'feminine.'[59]

The influence of the normative order in social lives implies that human beings not only act on it, but it reflects and passes judgment on their acts.[60] Thus the construction of women's identity is shaped by the culture and the society in which she lives.

4.7. Powers of Violence, Position in Relation to Identity

Power is used by people/groups to assert dominance, enforce subjugation and to exploit others who are different from them.[61] Violence here takes shape in the forms of physical, mental and emotional abuse. To perceive women as an object is violence in its worst form, because it totally negates the other aspects of woman's competence, and reins her in ways that she does not desire, and only allows her to do those things that have been approved by certain so

57 Sen, "Subordination and Sexual Control: A Comparative View of the Control of Women," 144.

58 Elizabeth Grosz, "Notes Towards a Corporeal Feminism," *Australian Feminist Studies* 5 (1987), 15.

59 Jean Baker Miller, *Towards a New Psychology of Women* (Boston: Beacon Press, 1976), 8-9.

60 Kingsley Davies, *Human Society* (Delhi: Surjeet Publications, 1981), 54.

61 Dulcie Abraham, "Gender Violence," *In God's Image* 13, no. 3 (Autumn 1994), 4.

called 'norms.' Violence is taken as demonstration of force and power against the other person. Thus, it becomes monologue, which treats the other person as an object to be manipulated and exploited.[62]

It is noticed that, norms are not applied equally to all members of a society, nor to all situations, they are rather adjusted according, to the positions people hold in the social order, their occupation, and the like. What is proper for a woman is not always proper for a man. Therefore, expectations and performances are always qualified in view of the socially defined situations in which the norm applies.[63] Sex differences have been among one of the basis for the ascriptions of lifetime status, which is why in every society, it is utilised not only for assigning definite statures but also for giving monopolies on achieved statures.[64] Feminism contributes to Christian understandings of human identity by probing the implications of gender and sexuality for the construal of personhood, and for social systems in which identities are shaped and expressed.[65]

Gender ideology explains the difference between men and women in terms of rights, obligations, responsibilities and rewards.Feminism asserts the right understanding of gender because gender differences have been manipulated and exploited for the benefit of some by oppressing the others.[66] Feminism recognizes the play of power in identity formation. In interacting situation, there is the identity of each person, which is supposedly not the same. This identity refers to ones positions and status within the social structure, which establishes ones rights and obligation with reference to others within the same structure. One's identity in a particular situation results from all the other position, he/she holds in other major social structures.[67] The

62 Sarojini Henry, "Violence against Women," in *Envisioning a New Heaven and a New Earth*, ed. Laarinawmi Ralte et al. (Delhi: ISPCK, 1998), 165.

63 Davies, *Human Society,* 56.

64 *Ibid.*, 99.

65 Christine Firer-Hinze, "Identity in Feminist Theological Debate," *Concilium* 2 (2000), 112.

66 *Ibid.*, 113-114.

67 Davies, *Human Society*, 85-86.

distribution of power is intimately bound up with the distribution of statuses and offices, and hence, with the configuration of status and strata: their social structure may be viewed as a legitimate power system.[68] The elite creates an ideology that protects and legitimises their own status, and gender relevant social definitions that devalue woman and feminity, and therefore labelling behaviour for both men and women. [69]According to Dubisch,

> Ideas of male and female, inside and outside, are related to conceptions of self and to one's experiences as a member of certain social groups in their relations with other social groups...concepts of gender are simply the framework upon which are hung important social values, as well as expressions and interpretations of life and society. It is through such opposition of female/male, inside/outside, public/private, intimacy/separation, self/other that people construct a language for talking about and reconciling the diverse experience of their lives, experiences that include life and death, sin and salvation, superiority and subordination, competition and commonality.[70]

Michael Foucault's explanation of how power works in social processes is central to the theoretical understanding of this perspective. His concern on power focuses on the knowledge of power matrix where people exert control through the various cultural practices, extending from personal relations to institutional centres of power. This is so "because power and politics in society, where confinement is so dominant, impinges upon the human body on which it is exercised, power is found to be the motive for bodily activity that is productivity, which in turn produces power."[71]

68 Davies, *Human Society*, 95.

69 *Ibid.,* 138.

70 J. Dubisch, ed., *Gender and Power in Rural Greece* (Princeton: Princeton University, 1986), 35-37.

71 Robert Wuthnow et al. ed., *Cultural Analysis: The Work of Peter L. Berger, Mary Doughlas, Michael Foucault and Jurgen Habermans* (New York: Routledge &

Articulation of human identity in relation to gender must be framed by struggle for right understanding and practice concerning marginalisation.[72] Men have power in a patriarchal society and the women are marginalized, therefore the views of men become dominant.

4.8. The Construction of the Identity of Esther and Vashti

Culture and society constructs the identity of women by inscribing the body of women, as docile and submissive. The context in which Vashti and Esther lived, and the present context may differ, but the objectification of women still exist. The patriarchal power continues to shape and influence the community. A woman is regarded as weaker despite her capabilities. Many a time, she is not looked at as another human being with qualities, but rather labelled as a mere 'woman.' Her body influences her identity in relation to other persons in the community.

The models of behaviour for male and female are seen in the Book of Esther. It is clear that society rewards men for being direct and aggressive, while it condemns women like Vashti, for equivalent behaviour. In one sense Mordecai and Vashti behave identically: both refused to debase themselves by submitting to illegitimate demands. This inspires praise of Mordecai but condemnation of Vashti.[73]

The women in the story conceal different identities, but each one is the product of patriarchal culture, each function in relationship to the men in the world. Vashti 'wins' by losing. She triumphs over patriarchal domination and control. Esther 'wins' by playing the man's game, which puts her in a position to work for her people.[74]

In contrast to Vashti, who refused to be men's sexual object and her husband's toy, Esther is seen as a stereotyped woman in a

---

Kegan Paul Ltd., 1987), 176.

72 Firer-Hinze, "Identity in Feminist Theological Debate," 117.

73 Mary Gendler, "The Restoration of Vashti," in *The Jewish Women: New Perspectives*, ed. Elizabeth Koltun (New York: Shocken Books, 1976), 158.

74 Alice Laffy, *An Introduction to the Old Testament: A Feminist Perspective* (Philadelphia: Fortress Press, 1988), 217.

man's world.[75] Perhaps this criticism is a bit harsh on Esther, since usually she is not held up as a model, whereas Vashti, when she is remembered, tends to be disparaged. Chief among the criticism of the historical critical method by liberation scholars has been the fallacy and fraudulent nature of claims for an 'objective' versus 'subjective' reading of biblical texts. No interpreter is able to divest herself of her values and assumptions, and then all interpretation of data and texts reflects to some degree the subjective predispositions of the interpreters.[76] Thus, the only way to read into these two characters is by letting no patriarchal value influence the interpretation.

Earlier we have seen how patriarchy gives men access to all the powers in the world, thus objectifying Vashti and Esther. The patriarchal society made their bodies, their identity, on which the men exercised their power, confining them to mere objects. Both the women in the story were not given the freedom to do what was right, because their whole life was ruled by men and their ideology regarding theroles of women.[77] Every human being has the right to one's own body, but such right was forbidden when Vashti attempted to use it in freedom. For this, she was never allowed to appear before the king and stripped off her crown. Esther on the other hand, conformed to the demands of men, but Esther's obedience cannot be viewed as submissiveness because in a land ruled by men where women were treated as chattels, she had no alternative but to comply with the demands of men. Her role should be understood as the one who shrewdly knew how the patriarchal structures functioned, so therefore appeared to have been under its authority, obediently.

75 Alice Laffy, *An Introduction to the Old Testament: A Feminist Perspective* (Philadelphia: Fortress Press, 1988), 216.

76 Renita Weems, "Womanist Reflections on Biblical Hermeneutics," in *Black Theology: A Documentary History*, Vol. 2, eds. James H. Cone & Gayraud S. Wilmore (Maryknoll: Orbis Books, 1993), 217.

77 Vashti was asked to appear before the king and the drunken courtier so that they might enjoy her beauty. Esther was subjected to a beautiful body where the king and all men in the harem found favour on her. In this Esther had no power to resist because of its dominant structure that forbids her to decide herself.

The present age still confines women's identity to an object which society can enjoy. In the political, social, economic, religious spheres, women are still perceived as incapable of accomplishing anything, except to tend homes and children.

Vashti and Esther were victims of the same Patriarchal power. When Vashti was ordered by the king, he expected from her perfect obedience, she was not consulted, neither was she called to be a part of the enjoyment nor share her opinion on the various aspects of the kingdom. But, she was a mere object to be shared and enjoyed. Likewise, Esther was neither asked her opinion as to whether she wanted to be the queen, rather her uncle forced her to join the harem. Women today still suffer such kind of violence, where women are told what to do and what not to do.

The violence experienced by Esther and Vashti parallels the violence that women face today. Women may not be asked to appear naked or to be exposed before men, yet when they are restricted and controlled under certain assumptions and roles assigned to them, it proves similar. In all these it is the male who exerts power over the female where the female becomes a mere thing to be used and stamped upon.

4.9. Implications for Re-Reading the Identity of Vashti and Esther in Today's Context

Reading the Book of Esther with a fresh perspective moves us to realise that power has been used as instrumental in violating the identity and dignity of women. It is a fact that women are physically different from men that makes room for such violence. A new perspective of the body seeks to go beyond the socially constructed roles, and puts emphasison the human's purpose of creation and its capability to reflect God's image in all things, calling for a celebration of differences. Thus re-reading the Bible, without the male bias becomesan important way of respecting one another and valuing the purpose of God's creation.

The traditional interpretation of the Bible is a one sided, and male dominated interpretation. Thus, it is important to re-read and reinterpret the Bible from women's perspectives in order to recover fully from the hidden roles and status of women.[78] It is hard for an individual to breakaway from tradition that has shaped their identity. Women are restricted and controlled under certain assumptions and roles assigned to them. The story of Vashti should be used as an example to challenge anything that oppresses them and limits their capabilities. Vashti shows us that what is important is one's dignity and self-respect. The story of Esther should not be remembered as a body that attracted the king, but as one who cleverly knew how patriarchy worked, and so complying with its wishes she becomes a Queen who will always be remembered for saving her people. Thus, we re-read the Book of Esther and interpret it from a different perspective giving both Vashti and Esther a positive identity, dominated by male identity. Doing this results in the implication of interpreting the present women's action and roles away from traditional understanding, which will give women freedom to decide for themselves.

In re-reading the Book of Esther the traditional interpretation of Vashti as a negative role model must be done away and Esther must be portrayed as a liberative model for women. Esther must not only be seen as positive because she did what was told, but she should also be seen beyond this image. She portrays a liberative model in her act of gaining the trust of the men and in her act of saving her people she represent one who is intelligent, brave and responsible. In re-reading we discern how the male bias interprets Esther and Vashti's role. This gives us the clue that the values of what are good and bad for women are socially constructed by patriarchy. Thus, the cultural and social understanding of women as a labeled body needs to be challenged. By criticizing tradition and culture we may find elements of a positive nature, which can be used to empower them. Tradition was made by people and is for people thus we need to be critical and challenge those traditions that are biased. Patriarchal values must not

78 Limala Longkumer, "Women in Ministry: A Reflection From Ao Naga Women," *In God's Image* 19, no. 4 (Dec 2000): 40.

be assigned to understand and judge the actions and roles of women as either bad or good.

Lastly, the story of Vashti shows us how the feminist movement began right from the time of biblical history. Today, as we live in a smaller world we become more aware of our needs, each person needs to be responsible to take that step to stop injustice. It's not about waiting for others to make that first courageous step, but we must dare to stand up against what we think is wrong. Vashti transgressed the boundaries of the patriarchal structure of her time because she did not want to lose her self-respect. Esther through her role as a queen can be seen as a story of a successful woman in a world dominated by men. This implies that women must dare to be different and must come out of any oppressive structure that forbids them to move forward.

Summary

The identity of women is always equated with sexuality. Men looked at women as mere sex objects. This has been the culture of society everywhere. The construction of women's body as a sex object leads to exercise men's power of violence, position and power in society that results to the inequality of the sexes. This has implications for women's identity because identity is connected to the value or worth of a person. Such conception calls us to compare the identity of Esther and Vashti, who in their time had been confined to such identities. Thus it calls for a re-reading of these two identities from the feminist point of view.

Identity is the most an important issue which effects all people irrespective of age, sex and race. Unless a person is given a chance to have an identity that reflects respects and equality, no matter what that person does, people will always equate this with the identity he/she carries. Since most people respect others for one's identity and not by one does. So, no matter how much one achieves, if the identity of that person is negative in the eyes of the people, this achievement is not always acknowledged. So, women's fight for a respectable identity is a basic need and right.

Women have always been ignored in the history of human kind except for few tales of women and usually those tales are negative. Women cannot accept and pretend that all the injustices exist because women are destined for it or that tradition must always be followed. The example of Vashti and Esther should inspire women to challenge oppressive authority fearless of the consequences. This re-reading of the identity of Esther and Vashti is not only to recover and unearth the true identity of these two women alone. But it also becomes a way of indicating to us that there are other characters in the Bible whose identity have been suppressed and therefore needs to be brought out and studied critically. Further more, it also implies that this same method of viewing women's identity should be applied at present for women's situation and needs.

Conclusion

The Bible is undoubtedly patriarchal in origins and thought; their particular patriarchal expressions being determined by social situations and historical circumstances. Patriarchy closely associated with hierarchy, is a way of ordering reality whereby male sex is understood to be superior to the female sex. This way of understanding the variation of the identity of men and women, men are consequently depicted as more competent, responsible, braver, intelligent, more rational, better suited for management and leadership. Usually oppression is obvious in a patriarchal culture. Role delineation makes certain attitudes, types of behaviour and occupations stereotypically acceptable for females and extols those roles while at the same time denying women other forms of behaviour considered appropriate 'for men only'. Sexual role stereotyping has been legitimated by many religions for thousands of years. This has affected even the present perception of women and their roles in societies.

Re-reading the Bible thus becomes a way of breaking away from the traditional and stereotyping of women's identity. The text and its stories, characters and events are looked at with perception with the aim of empowering women. It rejects all standards of judgment set by patriarchal culture. Thus it brings out the identity of women, which has been suppressed by the patriarchal ideology and interpretation and it uses such images to empower women's identity today since biblical images have affected the way women has been projected in the present.

Women have had to live within the patriarchal constructed boundaries and it has not helped women to live as equal to men. Would it have helped if the Bible's traditional concept of authority and inspiration were not in question? Would it have done well if women felt they should have stuck to house keeping because that was assigned to them? There have been people who decided to transcend beyond their assigned roles, and because of which life had become easier for many other women.

In transcending the roles and functions assigned by patriarchy, we are doing three things; firstly we are rejecting anything that obstructs a person's right and freedom. Secondly we become examples for others though it may cause scandals, pains, if we believe in ourselves we inspire people and also we make it easier for the future generation to set out in that areas. This responsibility as a woman still continues for us today, each person need to take her responsibility seriously. Thirdly, by transcending anything that binds women in moving forward in their life, careers, purpose, aim, women are just claiming their rights and their identity as human beings.

The significance of the body is about a new relationship of respect and identity, where we accept the difference in each other and use these differences to bring out the best in humanity. This respect and identity includes the whole of the community as we relate to each other, and as we struggle to understand each other. Thus, the only way for a change in the identity of women is to go beyond the understanding of body as a mere object, and understand women as a person with their own unique identity and importance.

The basic human relationship is about I-thou, but in a patriarchal structure the relationship of men to women is in terms of I-it, where men have power and women are objects for men.[1] Thus, what is required here is conversion of the perspective of I-it to I-thou to have right relationship. This leads to the relationship of I-thou-we, which is about community relations where we come together with others

---

1 Martin Buber, *I and Thou*, trans. W. Kaufman (New York: Charles Scribner & Sons, 1970), 67.

and we are made to realize that we are accountable to others as part of a particular community.[2]

None should be judged by neither any preconceived ideas nor roles be forced on any person. Identity today should not be restricted within a preconceived boundary. Identity grows in its fullest form when it has freedom to thrive and explore. Each person should have the freedom to explore and grow as one chooses, no law or ideology is greater than the purpose of God's creation in God's image which can come through only by love and respect in its various forms.

2 Martin Buber, *I and Thou*, trans. W. Kaufman (New York: Charles Scribner & Sons, 1970), 28-29.

Bibliography

Books and Book Sections

Aichele, George, et al., eds. *The Postmodern Bible.* London: Yale University Press, 1995.

Ardener, E. "Belief and the Problem of Women." In *Perceiving Women*. Edited by S. Ardener, 1-17. London: Malaby, 1975.

Atwood, Margaret. "The Female Body." In *The Female Body: Figures, Styles, Speculations*. Edited by Laurence Goldstein, 2-3. Ann Arbor: University of Michigan Press, 1991.

Augustine and Henry Chadwick. *Confessions*. Oxford: Oxford University Press, 1998.

Augustine. "De Trinitate." *St. Augustine: On the Holy Trinity, Doctrinal Treatises, Moral, Moral Treatises. A Select Library of the Nicene and Post Nicene Fathers,* Vol. III. Edited by Philip Schaff, 1-228. Buffalo: The Christian Literature Company, 1887.

Bartky, Sandra Lee. "Foucault, Feminity, and the Modernization of Patriarchal Power." In *Feminism and Foucault, Reflections on Resistance*. Edited by Irene Diamond and Lee Quinbee, 25-45. Boston: Beacon Press, 1988.

Beal, Timothy K. "Tracing Esther's Beginning." In *A Feminist Companion to Esther, Judith and Susanna*. Edited by Athalya Brenner, 87-110. Sheffield: Sheffield Academic Press, 1995.

__________ "Esther." In *Berit Olam: Studies in Hebrew Narrative and Poetry*. Edited by David W. Cotter, Collegevill: Liturgical Press, 1999.

Bellis, Alice Ogden. *Helpmates, Harlots, Heroes: Women's Stories in the Hebrew Bible.* Louisville: Westminster John Knox Press, 1994.

Berger, J. *Ways of Seeing.* London: Penguin Books, 1972.

Bickerman, Elias. *Four Strange Books of the Bible: Jonah, Daniel, Koheleth, Esther.* New York: Schocken Books, 1967.

Bingemer, Maria Clara. "Women in the Future of the Theology of Liberation." In *Feminist Theology from the Third World: A Reader.* Edited by Ursula King, 308-317. Maryknoll: Orbis Books, 1994.

Bird, Phyllis A. "Images of Women in the Old Testament." In *Religion and Sexism: Images of Woman in the Jewish and Christian Tradition.* Edited by Rosemary Radford Ruether, 41-88. New York: Simon & Schuster, 1974.

__________ "Images of Women in the Old Testament." In *The Bible and Liberation: Political and Social Hermeneutics.* Edited by Gottwald Norman, 250-306. Maryknoll: Orbis Books, 1983.

Brenner, Athalya. *The Israelite Women: Social Role in Literary Type in Biblical Narrative.* Sheffield: JSOT Press, 1985.

Brockington, L. H. *Ezra, Nehemiah, Esther.* London: Thomas Nelson & Sons Limited, 1969.

Bronner, Leila Leah. "Esther Revisited: An Aggadic Approach." In *A Feminist Companion to Esther, Judith and Susanna.* Edited by Athalya Brenner, 176-197. Sheffield: Sheffield Academic Press, 1995.

Brooton, Bernadette. *Brown Judaic Studies* 36. Chico: Scholars Press, 1982.

Buber, Martin. *I and Thou.* Translated by W. Kaufman. New York: Charles Scribner & Sons, 1970.

Chafetz, Janet Saltzman. "Gender Equality: Toward a Theory of Change." In *Feminism and Sociological Theory*. Edited by Ruth A.

Wallace, 135-160. Newbury Park, London, and New Delhi: Sage Publications, 1989.

Chyrsostom, John. "Discourse 2 on Genesis"; and "The Kind of Women who ought to be taken as Wives." In *Women in the Early Church*. Edited by Elizabeth A. Clark, 34-36. Minnesota: The Liturgical Press, 1983.

Clifford, Anne M. *Introducing Feminist Theology.* Maryknoll: Orbis Books, 2001.

Clines, David J. A. *The Esther Scroll: The Story of the Story*. Sheffield: University of Sheffield, 1984.

Collins, Adela Yarbro. "Introduction." In *Feminist Perspectives on Biblical Scholarship*. Edited by Adela Yarbro Collins, 1-10. Chico: Scholar Press, 1985.

__________ *Helpmates, Harlots, Heroes: Women's Stories in the Hebrew Bible.* Louisville: Westminster John Knox Press, 1994.

Comstock, Gary David. *Gay Theology without Apology.* Cleveland: Pilgrim Press, 1993.

Crawford, Sidnie White. "Esther: A Feminine Model for Jewish Diaspora." In *Gender and Difference in Ancient Israel.* Edited by Peggy L. Day, 161-171. Philadelphia: Fortress Press, 1989.

__________ "Esther," In *Women in Scripture: A Dictionary of Named and Unnamed Women in the Hebrew Bible. The Apocryphal/ Deuterocanonical Books and The New Testament.* Boston: Houghton Mifflin, 2000.

Culler, Jonathan. *On Deconstruction: Theory and Criticism after Structuralism*. London: Routledge & Kegan Paul, 1983.

Cyprian. "On the Dress of Virgins." In *Cyprian. A Select Library of the Nicene and Post Nicene Fathers*. Edited by Philip Schaff, 4:31. Grand Rapids, MI: William B. Eerdmans Publishing Company, 1956.

Daly, Mary. *Gyn/Ecology: The Metaethics of Radical Feminism*. London: The Women's Press, 1987.

Danby, Herbert. *The Mishnah.* Oxford: Clarendon Press 1933.

Davies, Kingsley. *Human Society.* Delhi: Surjeet Publications, 1981.

De Troyer, Kristian. "An Oriental Beauty Parlour: An Analysis of Esther 2.8-18 in the Hebrew, the Septuagint and the Second Greek Text." In *A Feminist Companion to Esther, Judith and Susanna*. Edited by Athalya Brenner, 47-70. Sheffield: Sheffield Academic Press, 1995.

Dietrich, Gabriele. *A New Thing on Earth: Hopes and Fears Facing Feminist Theology.* Delhi: ISPCK, 2001.

Dockery, David S. *Christian Scripture: An Evangelical Perspective on Inspirations, Authority and Interpretation.* Nashville: Broadman & Holman Publisher, 1995.

Dubisch, J., ed. *Gender and Power in Rural Greece.* Princeton: Princeton University, 1986.

Duff, Mildred and Noel Hope. *Esther, the Queen, on Life in the Ancient Palace of Shushan.* London, Edinburgh and New York: Marshall Brothers Ltd., n.d.

Eichrodt, W. *Theology of the Old Testament.* London: SCM Press Ltd., 1961.

Erikson, Erik H. *A Way of Looking at Things*. Edited by Stephen Schlein. New York: Norton & Company, 1987.

Evans, Mary J. E. *Woman in the Bible.* Carlisle: Paternoster Press, 1983.

Ewen, Robert B. *An Introduction to Theories of Personality*, Third Edition. New Jersey: Lawrence Erlbaum Associates Publishers, 1988.

Exum, J. Cheryl. "You shall let Every Daughter live: A Study of Exodus1: 8-2:10." In *The Bible and Feminist*. Edited by M. A. Tolbert, 161-179. Chico: Scholars Press, 1983.

Faye, Richard N. *The Heritage of Persia.* New York: Mentor Books, 1966.

Fenton, Natalie. "Feminism and Popular Culture." In *The Routledge Companion to Feminism and Post Feminism*. Edited by Sarah Gamble, 104-116. London & New York: Routledge, 2001.

Ferguson, Everett. *Backgrounds of Early Christianity.* Grand Rapids, MI: William B. Eerdmans Publishing Company, 1993.

Fiorenza, Elisabeth Schüssler. *Wisdom Ways: Introducing Feminist Biblical Interpretation.* Maryknoll: Orbis Books, 2001.

__________ "Remembering the Past in Creating the Future: Historical-Critical Scholarship and Feminist Biblical Interpretation." In *Feminist Perspectives on Biblical Scholarship.* Edited by Collins, 43-63. Adela Yarbro. Chico: Scholar Press, 1985.

__________ "Transforming the Legacy of Women's Bible." In *Searching the Scripture: A Feminist Introduction,* Vol.1. Edited by Elisabeth Shüssler Fiorenza, 1-21. London: SCM Press Ltd., 1994.

__________ and M. Shawn Copeland. *Violence against Women.* London: SCM Press Ltd., Maryknoll: Orbis Books, 1994.

__________ *Bread not Stone: The Challenges of Feminist Biblical Interpretation.* Boston: Beacon Press, 1995.

__________ *In Memory of Her: A Feminist Theological Reconstruction of Christian Origins.* New York: Cross Roads, 2002.

Foucault Michel, *History of Sexuality: An Introduction,* Vol. 1. New York: Vintage Books, 1990.

Fox, M. V. *Character and Ideology in the Book of Esther.* Columbia, University of South Carolina, 1991.

Frick, Frank S. *A Journey through the Hebrew Scripture.* Fort Worth, Philadelphia, San Diego, New York, Orlando, Austin, San Antonio, Toronto, Montreal, London, Sydney, Tokyo: Harcourt Brace College Publishers, 1995.

Fruech, Joanna. *Erotic Faculties.* Berkley & Los Ageles: University of California Press, 1996.

Gadamar, Hans-Georg. *Truth and Method.* New York: Crossroad, 1989.

__________ *Philosophical Hermeneutics.* Translated & Edited by David E. Linge. California: University of California Press, 1976.

Gamble, Sarah. *The Routledge Companion to Feminism and Post Feminism.* London & New York: Routledge, 2001.

Gendler, Mary. "The Restoration of Vashti." *The Jewish Woman.* Edited by Elizabeth Koltun, 241-247. New York: Schochen Books, 1976.

Ghrishman, R. *Iran.* Suffolk: Richard Clay & Company Ltd., 1954.

Ginzberg, L. *The Legends of the Jews.* Philadelphia: Jewish Publication Society, 1941.

Graham, Ealine. *Making the Difference, Gender, Personhood and Theology*. New York: Mowbray, 1995.

Grant, Robert and David Tracy, A *Short History of the Interpretation of the Bible,* Philadelphia: Fortress Press, 1984.

Grosz, Elizabeth. "Bodies and Knowledge: Feminism and the Crisis of Reason." In *Feminist Epistemologies.* Edited by Linda Alcoff & Elizabeth Potter, 195-202. New York, Routledge, 1993.

Henry, Sarojini. "Violence against Women." In *Envisioning a New Heaven and a New Earth.* Edited by Lalrinawmi Ralte, et al, 165-169. Delhi: ISPCK, 1998.

Herodotus. *The Histories.* Translated by Aubrey de Selincourt. Suffolk: Penguin Books Ltd., 1965.

Hetherington, K. *Expressions of Identity: Space, Performance Politics.* New Delhi: Sage Publications, 1998.

Irigaray, L. *This Sex is not One.* Ithaca: Cornell University Press, 1985.

Jacobs, Michael. *Sigmund Freud.* New Delhi: Sage Publications, 1992.

Keil, C. F. *Esther.* Grand Rapids, Grand Rapids, MI: William B. Eerdmans Publishing Company, 1980.

Kent, Charles Foster. *A History of Jewish People.* London: Smith, Elder & Co, 1912.

Klein, Lillian R. "Honour and Shame." In *A Feminist Companion to Esther, Judith and Susanna.* Edited by Athalya Brenner, 149-175. Sheffield: Sheffield Academic Press, 1995.

Knight, A. F. *Esther, Song of Songs, Lamentations: Introduction and Commentary.* London: SCM Press Ltd., 1955.

Kuhn, A. *The Power of Image: Essays on Representation and Sexuality.* London & Boston: Routledge & Kegan Paul, 1985.

Laffey, Alice L. *Wives, Harlots and Concubines: The Old Testament in Feminist Perspectives.* Philadelphia: Fortress Press, 1988.

__________ *An Introduction to the Old Testament: A Feminist Perspective.* Philadelphia: Fortress Press, 1988.

Laniak, Timothy S. *Honour and Shame in the Book of Esther.* Atlanta: Scholars Press, 1998.

Leslie, Julia and Mary McGee, ed. *Invented Identities: The Interplay of Gender, Religion and Politics in India.* New Delhi: Oxford University Press, 2000.

Lipton, Diana. "The Woman's Lot in Esther." In *Bodies, Lives, Voices: Gender in Theology.* Edited by Kathleen O'Grady, et al. Sheffield: Sheffield Academic Press 1998.

Machaffie, Barbara J. *Her Story: Women in Christian Tradition.* London: A & C Black, 1986.

Masenya, Mmadipoane (Ngwana 'Mphahlele). "Esther and Northen Sotho Stories and an African-South African Women's Commentary." In *Other Ways of African Woman and the Bible.* Edited by Musa W. Dube, 20-35. Society of Biblical Literature Atlanta: Geneva: WCC Publications, 2001.

McDowell, Linda and Rosemary Pringle, eds. *Defining Women: Social Institutions and Gender Divisions.* Oxford: Polity Press & Blackwell Publishers, 1992.

McKenzie, J. L. *A Theology of the Old Testament.* New York: Chapman, 1974.

Miles, Margaret R. *Carnal Knowing.* New York: Vintage, 1991.

Miller, Jean Baker. *Towards a New Psychology of Women.* Boston: Beacon Press, 1976.

Mills, S. *Feminist Stylistics.* New York: Routledge, 1995.

Neusner, Jacob. *The Components of the Rabbinic Documents from the Whole to the Parts. 11, Esther Rabbah 1.* Atlanta: USF Academy Commentary Series, 1997.

Niditch, Susan. "Esther: Folklore, Wisdom, Feminism and Authority." In *A Feminist Companion to Esther, Judith and Susanna.* Edited by Athalya Brenner, 26-46. Sheffield: Sheffield Academic Press, 1995.

Olmstead, A. T. *History of the Persian Empire.* Chicago: Chicago Press, 1966.

Pardes, Iiana. *Counter Traditions in the Bible: A Feminist Approach.* London: Harvard University Press, 1993.

Pathrapankal, Joseph. *Text and Context: In Biblical Interpretation.* Bangalore: Dharmaram Publication, 1993.

Paulo, Freire. *Pedagogy of the Oppressed.* New York: Herder & Herder, 1971.

Pedersen, J. *Israel: Its Life and Culture.* London: Oxford University Press, 1926.

Phipps, W. E. *Assertive Biblical Women.* Westport, CT & London: Greenwood Press, 1992.

Price Ira Maurice, Ovid R. Selles and E. Leslie Carlson. *The Monuments and the Old Testament.* Philadelphia: The Judson Press, 1958.

Pui–Lan, Kwok. "Racism and Ethnocentrism in Feminist Biblical Interpretation." In *Searching the Scriptures: A Feminist Introduction.* Edited by Elisabeth Schüssler Fiorenza, 101-116. New York: Crossroad Publishing, 1993.

__________ *Discovering the Bible in the Non-Biblical World.* Maryknoll: Orbis Books, 1995.

Rajan, Rajeshwari Sunder. *Real and Imagined Woman: Gender, Culture and Post Colonialism.* New York & London: Routledge, 1993.

Rebera, Ranjini. "Challenging Patriarchy." In *Feminist Theology from the Third World: A Reader.* Edited by Ursula King, 105-113. Maryknoll: Orbis Books, 1994.

Ricciotti, G. *The History of Israel,* Vol. 2. Milwaukee: Bruce, 1955.

Root, J. *Pictures of Women: Sexuality.* London & Boston: Pandora Press, 1984.

Rossi, Alice S. "Preface: Feminist Lives and Works." In *The Feminist Papers: From Adams to De Beauvior*. Edited by A. S. Rossi, IX-XIX. New York/London: Columbia University Press, 1973.

Roy, Ashik. *Selling Stereotypes: Images of Women in Indian Television.* New Delhi: New Concepts Information Systems Pvt. Ltd., 1998.

Ruether, Rosemary Radford. *Sexism and God Talk: Towards a Feminist Theology.* Boston: Beacon Press, 1983.

__________ "Feminist Interpretation: A Method of Correlation." In *Feminist Interpretation of the Bible*. Edited by Letty M. Russell, 111-124. Philadelphia: Westminster Press, 1985.

Sanday, Peggy Reeves. *Female Power and Male Dominance: On the Origins of Sexual Inequality.* New York: Cambridge University. 1981.

Sangari, Kumkum and Sudesh Vaid, eds. *Recasting Women: Essays in Colonial History.* New Delhi: Kali for Women, 1989.

Sasson, J. M, "Esther." In *The Literary Guide to the Bible*. Edited by R. Alter & F. Kermode, 335-342. Cambridge: Harvard University Press, 1987.

Scanzoni, Letha and Nancy Hardesty. *All We're Meant to Be: A Biblical Approach to Women's Liberation.* Waco: Word Books, 1975.

Schleiermacher, F. D. E. *Hermeneutic: The Handwritten Manuscripts.* Translated by J. Duke and J. Forstman. Edited by Heinz Kimmerle. Missoula: Scholars Press, 1977.

Sen, Gita. "Subordination and Sexual Control: A Comparative View of the Control of Women." In *The Women Gender and Development Reader*. Edited by Malini Visvanathan, et al, 142-149. New Delhi: Zubaan, 1997.

Sickle, C. E. Van. *A Political and Cultural History of Ancient World.* Boston: Houghton Wifflin, 1947.

Spender, Dale. *Man Made Language.* London: Routledge & Kegan Paul, 1985.

Stannard, U. "The Mask of Beauty." In *Woman in Sexist Society: Studies in Power and Powerlessness.* Edited by V. Gornick and B. K. Moran, 187-203. New York: Basic Books, Inc., 1971.

Stendahl, Kristen. *The Bible and the Role of Women.* Translated by Emilie T. Sander. Philadelphia: Fortress Press, 1966.

Swindler, Leonard. *Biblical Affirmation of Woman.* Philadelphia: The Westminster Press, 1979.

Tamez, Elsa, "Women's Re-reading of the Bible," In *Feminist Theology from the Third World: A Reader.* Edited by Ursula King, 190-201. Maryknoll: Orbis Books, 1994.

Tertullian. "On the Apparel of Women." In *Fathers of the Third Century: Tertullian Part Four, Minucuis, Conumodian, Origin, Part First and Second. The Ante-Nicene Father,* Vol. IV. Edited by Roberts Alexander and James Donaldson. Revised by A. Cleveland Coxe, 14-26. New York: Charles Scribner's Sons, 1913.

__________ "On the Dress of Women." In *Women in the Early Church. Message of the Fathers of the Church 13.* Translated by Elizabeth A. Clark. College Ville, 38. Minnesota: The Liturgical Press, 1983.

Thapan, Menakshi. "Gender and Embodiment in Everyday Life." In *Embodiment: Essays on Gender and Identity.* Edited by M. Thapan, 1-26. New Delhi: Oxford University Press, 1997.

Trible, Phyllis. *God and the Rhetoric of Sexuality.* Philadelphia: Fortress Press, 1978.

__________ *Texts of Terror: Literary – Feminist Readings of Biblical Narratives.* Philadelphia: Fortress Press, 1984.

Troyer, Kristin De, "An Oriental Beauty Parlour: An Analysis of Esther 2.8-18 in the Hebrew, the Septuagint and the Second Greek Text." In *A Feminist Companion to Esther, Judith and Susanna.* Edited by Athalya Brenner, 47-70. Sheffield: Sheffield Academic Press, 1995.

Viswanath, Kalpana. "Shame and Control: Sexuality and Power in Feminist Discourse in India." In *Embodiment: Essays on Gender and Identity.* Edited by M. Thapan, 313-333. New Delhi: Oxford University Press, 1997. 313-333.

Vos, C. J. *Women in the Old Testament Worship.* Delft: Judels and Brinkman, 1968.

Weems, Renita J. *Just a Sister Away: A Womanist Vision of Women's Relationships in the Bible.* San Diego: Lura Media 1988.

__________ "Reading her Ways through the Struggle." In *Stony the Road we Trod: African American Biblical Interpretation.* Edited by Cane Hope Felder, 71-78. Philadelphia: Fortress Press, 1991.

__________ "Womanist Reflections on Biblical Hermeneutics." In *Black Theology: A Documentary History*, Vol. 2. Edited by James H. Cone and Gayraud S. Wilmore, 216-224. Maryknoll: Orbis Books, 1993.

Weisner, Mary. "Luther and Women: The Death of Two Marys." In *Feminist Theology: A Reader.* Edited by Ann Loades, 123-137. Louisville: SPCK, 1990.

Wendell, Elisabeth Moltmann. *A Land Flowing with Milk and Honey: Perspectives on Feminist Theology.* New York: Crossroad, 1986.

White, Pamela Copper. *The Cry of Tamar: Violence against Women and the Church's Response.* Minneapolis: Fortress Press, 1995.

White, Sidnie. A. "Esther. A Feminine Model for Jewish Diaspora." In *Gender and Difference in Ancient Israel.* Edited by P. L. Day, 161-177. Minneapolis: Fortress Press, 1989.

Widengren, Geo. "The Persians." In *Peoples of Old Testament Times.* Edited by D. J. Wiseman, 326-327. Oxford: Clarendon Press, 1973.

Winter, Gibson. *Elements for Social Ethics: The Role of Social Science in Public Policy.* New York: The Macmillan Company, London: Collier-Macmillan Ltd., 1966.

Wither, J. Eugene. *Erikson Identity and Religion.* New York: The Seabury Press, 1982.

Wuthnow, Robert, et al. *Cultural Analysis: The Work of Peter L. Berger, Mary Doughlas, Michael Foucault and Jurgen Habermans.* New York: Routledge & Kegan Paul Ltd., 1987.

Wyler, Bea. "Esther: The Incomplete Emancipation of Queen." In *A Feminist Companion to Esther, Judith and Susanna*. Edited by Athalya Brenner, 111-135. Sheffield: Sheffield Academic Press, 1995.

Reference Works and Commentaries

Anderson, Bernhard W. "The Book of Esther." In *The Interpreters Bible,* Vol. 3. Edited by Nolan B. Halman, 824-825. Nashville: Abington Press, 1954.

Breneman, Mervin. "Esther." In *The New American Commentary: Ezra, Nehemiah and Esther,* Vol. 10. Edited by E. Ray Elendenen, 303-323. Nashville: Broadman & Holman Publishers, 1993.

Bush, Frederic. *"Esther."* In *WBC: Ruth and Esther*, Vol. 9. Edited by David A. Hubbard, et al, 338-370. Dallas: Word Books Publisher, 1996.

Crawford, Sidnie White. "The Book of Esther" In *The New Interpreters Bible: A Commentary in Twelve Volumes*, Vol. 111. Edited by Leander Eeck, et al., 855-892. Nashville: Abingdon Press, 1988.

____________ " Esther." In *The Women's Bible Commentary*. Edited by Carol A. Newsom and Sharon H. Ringe, 131-137. Louisville: Westminster John Knox Press, 1992.

Driver and Briggs. *The New Brown – Driver – Briggs – Gesenius Hebrew and English Lexicon*. Peabody, Massachusetts: Henduckson 1979.

Dumm, Demetrius R. "Tobit, Judith, Esther." In *New Jerome Biblical Commentary.* Edited by Raymond E. Brown, et. al, 628-632. Bangalore: TPI, 1999.

Fiorenza, Elizabeth Schüssler. "Feminist Hermeneutics." In *ABD* Vol. 2. Edited by D. N. Freedman, 783-791. New York: Double Day, 1992.

Grayson, A. Kirk. "Mesopotamia, History of." In *ABD*, Vol. 4. Edited by D. N. Freedman, 747-750. New York: Double Day, 1992.

Guthrie, Donald. *New Bible Dictionary.* Secunderabad: OM Books, 1962.

Howard, David M. "Esther: Theology of." In *The New International Dictionary of Old Testament Theology and Exegesis,* Vol. 4. Edited by Willem A. Van Gimeren, 582-585. Nashville: Paternoster Press, 1997.

Johnston, Gordon H. 'syrs' In *The New International Dictionary of Old Testament Theology and Exegesis,* Vol. 3. Edited by Willem A. Van Gimeren, 6244-6249. Nashville: Paternoster Press, 1997.

Moore, Carey A. "Esther, Book of." In *ABD,* Vol. 2. Edited by David Noel Freedman, 633-642. New York: Double Day, 1992.

__________ *Women in Scripture: A Dictionary of Named and Unnamed Women in The Hebrew Bible, The Apocryphal/ Deuterocanonical Books and the New Testament.* Edited by Carol Meyers, et al, 166-167. New York: Houghton Wifflin Company, 2000.

Paton, Lewis Bayles. *A Critical and Exegetical Commentary on the Book of Esther.* Edinburgh: T & T Clark, 1908.

Unger, Merrill F. *"Adar."* In *Ungers Bible Dictionary.* Edited by Merrill F. Unger, 20. Chicago: Moody Press, 1960.

Witton, Davis T., ed. *Ezra, Nehemiah, Esther: The Century Bible.* Edinburgh: TC & EC Jack. n.y.

Journal Articles

Bechtel, L. M. "Shame as a Sanction of Social Control in Biblical Israel: Judicial, Political and Social Shaming." *JSOT* 49 (Feb. 1991): 47-76.

Bickerman, E. J. "The Colphon of the Greek Book of Esther," *JBL* 63 (1944): 339-362.

Clines, D. J. "Possibilities and Priorities of Biblical Interpretation in an International Perspectives" *BIBLNT* 1(1993): 67-87.

Export, V. "The Real and its Double: The Body." *Discourse* 11 (1988): 3-27.

Exum, J. Cheryl. "The Mothers of Israel: The Patriarchal Narratives from a Feminist Perspective." *BIB Rev* 2 (1986): 60-64.

Feldman, Louis H. "'Josephus' Portrait of Ahasuerus." *Australian Biblical Review* XL, no. 11 (1994): 3-17.

Fiorenza, Elizabeth Schüssler. "The Ethics of Biblical Interpretation: De Centering Biblical Scholarship." *JBL* 107 (1988): 3-17.

Firer-Hinze Christine, "Identity in Feminist Theological Debate." *Concilium* 2 (2000): 113-120.

Gordis, Robert. "Studies, in the Esther Narrative." *JBL* 95 (1982): 43-58.

Grosz. Elizabeth. "Notes Towards a Corporeal Feminism." *Australian Feminist Studies* 5 (1987): 15-20.

Jackowski, Karol."Holy Disobedience in Esther." *Theology Today* XLV, no. 4 (Jan. 1989): 403-414.

Jones, Bruce W. "Two Misconceptions about the Book of Esther." *CBQ* XXXIX, no. 2 (April 1977): 171-181.

Longkumer, Limala. "Women in Ministry: A Reflection from Ao Naga Women." In *God's Image* 19, no. 4 (Dec. 2000): 40-41.

Mananzan, Mary John. "Feminist Socialization: Woman as Victims and Collaborators." *Concilium* 1 (1994): 6-7.

Meyers, Carol. "Procreation, Production, and Protection: Male-Female Balance in Early Israel. "*JAAR* 51 (1983): 569-593.

Polinska, Wioleta. "Dangerous Bodies: Women's Nakedness and Theology." *Journal of Feminist Studies in Religion* 16, no. 1 (Spring 2000): 45-62.

Rajkumar, Evangeline Anderson. "Significance of the 'Body' in Feminist Theological discourse." *Bangalore Theological Forum* XXXIII, no. 2 (Dec. 2001): 80-89.

Rogerson, J. W. "What does it mean to be Human? The Central Question of Old Testament Theology." *JSOT* 87 (1990): 285-298.

Sakenfeld, Katharine Doob. "Feminist Perspectives on Bible and Theology: An Introduction to Selected Issues and Literature." *Interpretation: A Journal of Bible and Theology* XLII, no. 1 (Jan. 1998): 5-18.

Sakenfeld, Katharine Doob. "Feminist Reading of The Bible: Problems and Promises." *BTF* XXX, no. 11 (Dec. 2000): 18-27.

Talmon, S. "Wisdom in the Book of Esther." *VT* 13 (1963): 419-455.

Trible, Phyllis. "Depatriarchalizing in Biblical Interpretation." *JAAR* XLI, no. 1 (March 1973): 30-48.

Yanni, D. A. "The Social Construction of Women as Mediated by Advertising." *Journal of Communication* 14 (1990): 71-81.

Webliography

www.english.upenn.edu/~lwarner/esth.html (accessed January 12, 2003).

www.torah.org/learning/yomtov/purim/5756/vol.1No.68.html (accessed January 12, 2003).

www.wujs.org.il/activist/activities/(programs/purim/esther/html (accessed January 12, 2003).

www.wujs.org.il/activist/activities/programs/purim/eappendix.html (accessed January 12, 2003).

Newspaper

Xavier, C. "Advertisements and Women," *Indian Express* 8,1992, 8.

Unpublished Work

Joseph Abraham, *Re-reading The Old Testament: A Study of Feminist Readings of Gen. 1-3,* A Thesis Submitted in Partial Fulfilment of the University's Requirement for the Degree of the Doctor of Philosophy, July 1996, Coventry University in Collaboration with Wycliffe Hall, Oxford, England.